Recent Research in Psychology

Sybe J. S. Terwee

Hermeneutics in Psychology and Psychoanalysis

Springer-Verlag
Berlin Heidelberg New York
London Paris Tokyo Hong Kong

Editor

Sybe J. S. Terwee
Leiden University, Faculty of Social Sciences
Unit of Experimental and Theoretical Psychology
P. O. Box 9555, 2300 RB Leiden, The Netherlands

ISBN-13:978-3-540-51806-8 e-ISBN-13:978-3-642-83984-9
DOI: 10.1007/978-3-642-83984-9

2126/3140-543210 –Printed on acid-free paper

CONTENTS

Preface

In the chapters which follow, I will discuss various subjects from a theoretical-psychological perspective. Though the discussion will not be restricted to a single discipline, but ranges from experimental psychology to psychoanalysis, in each case the focus of attention is the scientific status of the theories scrutinized. Earlier versions of four of the chapters have been published elsewhere. Chapter 1, "Psychology and Philosophy of Science", is an expanded version of a Dutch paper written for Van Strien and Van Rappard's volume on the foundations of psychology, *Grondvragen van de Psychologie*. Chapter 2, "The Early Reception of Psychoanalysis", has appeared in an almost identical form in Bem and Rappard's (1988) volume, *Studies in the History of the Social Sciences 5*. Chapter 3, "The Case of Johannes Linschoten's Apostasy: Phenomenological versus Empirical-Analytical Psychology", is an elaboration of the Dutch article, "Het essentialisme van Johannes Linschoten", published in *Psychologie en Maatschappij* in 1987. The substance of this chapter is considerably different from the earlier paper. Chapter 4, "Rhetorical Analysis and the Question of Relativism", was published in essentially the same form in a volume edited by W. Baker et al, *Recent Trends in Theoretical Psychology* (1988). It is based on an exchange of arguments with Kenneth J. Gergen at the 1987 meeting of the International Society for Theoretical Psychology in Banff, Canada. Chapter 5, "The Hermeneutical Conception of Psychoanalysis", is a rewritten version of a 1987 article in *Psychoanalysis and Contemporary Thought*, entitled "Grünbaum's Foundations of Psychoanalysis". Chapter 6, "The Uses of Hermeneutics for Psychology: The Case of Ergonomics", has benefited from discussions in the study group "Filosofie van de Mens- en Cultuurwetenschappen". I wish to thank the members of this group, philosophers and researchers in the humanities from different universities in the Netherlands, for their helpful comments on earlier Dutch versions of the chapter. A Dutch version will appear in a volume edited by Anton Mooij and Guy Widdershoven, members of the study group, entitled *Interpretatie in de Psychologie.* Chapter 7, "A Rhetorical Approach to Dream Theories and Dreams", has been newly written for the present volume. It is partly based on a paper presented to the European Association for the Study of Dreams 1988 Conference in London, and partly on a paper presented at the 1988 Cheiron Meeting in Budapest. I am grateful to many colleagues and friends -- I mention only Theo de Boer, Christine Van Boheemen, Kenneth Gergen, Paul Hoch, and the members of the Theoretical Psychology Department at Leiden University -- for their critical comments on earlier versions of parts of the manuscript, and for their encouragement and assistance at various stages of the project. Finally, I wish to thank Naomi Hylkema, Neline Ritsma, and Yvonne Weber from the Faculty of Social Sciences at Leiden, and Angie Pleit-Kuiper (Language Processing) for their kind assistance in the preparation of this manuscript for publication.

INTRODUCTION

The aim of this introduction is to provide an overview of the philosophical and methodological perspectives common in present-day psychology. Discussions between these perspectives may lead us to the theoretical problems of the foundations of psychology that form the subject of the first chapter. To start with, a few words will be said about the tension between two families of approaches in psychology (and related social and cultural sciences): the empirical-analytical and the empirical-hermeneutical approach. The major part of this book will consist of discussions between representatives of these approaches. What exactly is to be understood by empirical-analytical psychology and by hermeneutics?

The dominant view of scientific method in academic psychology has evolved out of logical-positivist philosophy as it was formulated at the beginning of this century in Vienna. Its ideal is a unified method for all sciences. This method is a logical consequence of the empirical-analytical approach to reality. It is assumed that reality may be broken up into logically independent variables. These variables are externally, but not internally, related: i.e., no meaning relations exist between them. External relations may have the character of universal laws or statistical correlations. A second assumption of empirical-analytical psychology is that such law-like relations between variables may be discovered in psychological reality. In this view, the aim of science is to provide theories consisting of general laws which enable us to explain, predict, and control phenomena. Within Dutch psychology, the empirical-analytical approach as outlined above has been introduced and expounded by J. Linschoten (1964) and A.D. de Groot (1961). But we can look at virtually any textbook on methodology in psychology to see these methods and their assumptions explained and defended.

It is important to distinguish between the empirical-analytical method as one of the possible methods of research in the sciences, and the empirical-analytical world view which claims that the structure of reality is such that it cannot be understood in any other way. As will be argued in a consideration of the work of Adolf Grünbaum in chapter 5, the adoption of this world view is not necessary for a scientist. I will also refer to Linschoten's arguments, presented in chapter 3, propagating empirical-analytical psychology, without falling into the trap of a scientistic world view. In other words, the empirical-analytical approach is useful for certain purposes, but it doesn't preclude the possibility of alternative approaches. There is a growing sensitivity in psychology to the necessity of alternative approaches: some of these will be outlined in sections 8-10 of the first chapter and analyzed in more detail in chapters 4 and 6 of this volume. Still speaking in very broad and generalized terms, the alternatives to the empirical-analytical approach may be subsumed under the term "hermeneutics"[1], which covers a family of related approaches to the interpretative character of psychology. These approaches share the following arguments that set them apart from empirical-analytical psychology:

(1) There is no need to analyze psychological reality into independent variables because we are familiar with it before any formal or scientific analysis. Since human experience is conditioned by internal relations, it is also doubtful whether such an empiricist analysis is useful for all purposes. It certainly involves a reduction and a subsequent disturbance of all sorts of internal relations and meanings in everyday life. As an example of an internal relation we may think of borrowing a book, followed by its return. If practical experience would show that books are seldom returned, the concept of 'borrowing' would gradually lose its meaning. In a Wittgensteinian spirit, we might say that meanings are only possible within forms of life and remain dependent on them: a change in everyday practice would lead to a change of meaning. It seems that internal (meaning) relations imply certain regularities, as was indeed indicated by Wittgenstein (1953). Empirical-analytical science concentrates on those regularities which may be measured and regarded as external relations without further ado. An experimental psychologist might look for the relationships existing between operationalizations like "borrowing behavior" and "returning behavior". Hermeneuticians acknowledge the legitimate character of such research. They are not denying the possibility of objective science. Their point is rather that an empiricist approach is not very fruitful in certain cases; and in any case, it is only one of the possible approaches. The hermeneutic approach aims

for knowledge without such reductive operations as those mentioned above. It consists of an orderly search for internal relations; the meaning of phenomena may become apparent if we look at their context and history. Hermeneutics constructs or reconstructs meaning relations between significant parts of the context and the context as a whole. More will be said about this in sections 8-10 of the first chapter. In chapter 6, an ergonomic explanation of accidents at sea will be scrutinized in order to provide an example of the hermeneutical approach. A quite different example of hermeneutic analysis will be presented in the rhetorical approach to dreams described in chapter 7.

(2) Hermeneuticians claim that explanations do not necessarily require laws. In explanations which do make use of laws (deductive-nomological explanations, see chapter 1, section 6), the phenomenon to be explained appears as the logical conclusion from a set of initial conditions and laws. It is a matter of debate whether this type of explanation is (implicitly) present in every possible scientific explanation. Hermeneuticians deny this. They claim that explanation is possible without recourse to laws. The contextual description of phenomena may lead to several types of explanation, such as narrative explanations (M. Gergen 1987), teleological explanations (C. Taylor 1971), motivational explanations (R.S. Peters 1958), and contextual explanations (Terwee 1983). In the field of ergonomics, a subdiscipline of psychology with an objective-scientific reputation (see chapter 6), it has been argued that a purposive model might be fruitful (Taylor 1976), and that an adequate framework for the understanding of accidents and safety behavior (Taylor 1987) may be found in hermeneutics.

It follows that hermeneuticians believe in the possibility of knowledge outside the realm of objective empirical-analytical science. There is no need for empirical psychology to reduce reality into abstract variables and to search for laws. I will claim in the following that several forms of hermeneutics may be fruitful approaches to psychology. The choice of theoretical frameworks and methods is free: to me it seems a pragmatic question which method is most appropriate for a given discipline or specialism. As will be shown in various contexts in this volume, there is a tendency in the social sciences to proclaim the empirical-analytical approach as the one and only scientific method. This, I argue, is the consequence of a foundationalist ontology and an unpractically narrow epistemology. In chapter 2, Freud's scientism forms the object of attention. In chapter 3, the arguments of the Dutch psychologist Linschoten are evaluated against an empirical-analytic world view. In chapter 4, I am mainly concerned with the problem of relativism that is usually associated with hermeneutics. Chapter 5 evaluates Adolf Grünbaum's rejection of the hermeneutical conception of psychoanalysis and his empirical-analytical world view. Chapters 6 and 7 provide examples of hermeneutical psychology, as mentioned above.

Finally, we may ask what hermeneutical theory has to say about existing forms of empirical-analytical psychology. On the one hand, interpretative methods may be seen as alternatives which could coexist peacefully with the empirical-analytical method. On the other hand, hermeneuticians have maintained that traditional empirical-analytical research is based on implicit interpretations. This attitude is found in the forceful rhetorical analyses of present-day theory by scholars such as Michael Billig, Kenneth Gergen, and Donald McCloskey. Their arguments are partly based on methodological principles, well-known to philosophers of science and generally accepted, for instance that the neutrality and objectivity of even the most exact research are dependent on fundamental choices such as theoretical framework (De Groot 1961), selective viewpoints (Duintjer 1969), and methods of research (Danziger 1985a). In other words, even the most objective research is dependent on interpretative choices which are often left implicit (Gergen 1982). This line of criticism forms the subject matter of a section on rhetorical approaches in the first chapter.

1

PSYCHOLOGY AND PHILOSOPHY OF SCIENCE

Contents:

1. *Philosophy of Science and its Relation to Psychology*

Most introductions to Philosophy of Science use a similar approach. They start with the development of philosophy of science in this century, including chapters on logical positivism, critical rationalism, the received view, Kuhn's theory of paradigms, and Lakatos' theory of research programs. Some books present arguments for and against methodological monism -- the view that one method should be used in all sciences. Relatively little attention is paid to the question what the proper methods for the humanities are (a German Introduction by Helmut Seiffert forms an exception). Work addressing that specific problem, like *Hermeneutics and Psychological Theory*, a volume edited by Messer, Woolfolk and Sass (1988), is usually not seen as belonging to the field of philosophy of science proper.

Philosophy of Science textbooks, in other words, mainly deal with the empirical-analytical approach. Since this method has been predominant in the social sciences for over a century now, it is remarkable that most of the examples are taken from the natural sciences. This is, of course, due to the fact that the social sciences are seen as less impressive in their scientific results and technological applications, and are sometimes called "immature". A Dutch introduction by G.H. de Vries (1984) is one of the few to analyze examples from sociology and psychology. In this chapter, the empirical-analytical method as it has been developed by several schools of philosophy of science, will be outlined first. The assumptions of empirical-analytical psychology will be explicated next. Then the approaches within the hermeneutical family will be scrutinized.

When discussing the views of some influential philosophers of science, I do so from a specific point of view. I am primarily interested in the specific ways in which those philosophers have exerted influence on psychology. I will also ask what contribution hermeneutics has made or might still make. Let me give an example to illustrate the differences resulting from the change of perspective I advocate.

A few introductions begin by expounding Aristotle's philosophy of science (cf. De Vries 1984, Losee 1979). They call Aristotle the first philosopher of science and view him as the precursor of classic natural science. Aristotle's ideas on deduction, induction, explanation, and causality, found in the *Analytica Posteriora*, are given attention. However, once we focus on the importance of Aristotle's thoughts on psychology, it seems reasonable to start from Aristotle's own views on the proper approach to understanding human life. According to him, human action belongs to the sphere of the variable, and it should not be approached in a scientific manner. The *Nicomachean Ethics* state that we use prudence (*phronesis*) in making practical decisions, and not some kind of scientific knowledge (*episteme*). Ethical or practical questions are not the domain of science. The distinction made by Aristotle between practical reason and scientific truth has not been influential so far in either empirical psychology or in philosophy of science. Both fields do not seem to be concerned with the specific forms of rationality attributed by Aristotle to human decision-making and judgment in ethics. Indeed, according to the Greeks these did not form a subject for science, and this classic categorization may serve as an excuse for histories of psychology and philosophy of science to persevere in their disregard of the *Ethics*. Yet it seems that Aristotle, in his treatment of these problems, has provided an essential framework which forms the basis for several modern discussions on the nature of psychological explanation (cf. Aristotle, NE, book VI; Widdershoven 1987, ch. 1). He explains that we cannot expect the same kind of exact knowledge in relation to human action as with regard to physical phenomena. Only in the latter case do we deal with the domain of the invariable and the necessary, which makes it possible to ask for mechanistic scientific explanations.

Modern philosophy of science, to the extent that it is still dominated by the ideal of a unified science of the Vienna Circle, is blind to approaches outside the borders of empirical-analytical method, and consequently must neglect Aristotle's *Ethics*. The explication of everyday deliberation, as Aristotle defines it, defies the necessity of reductionist analysis. Mainstream psychology exemplifies the same aversion towards Aristotle's philosophy of action. Historians of psychology, in their search for the roots of empirical psychology, refer to Aristotle's "associationism" (both historically and philosophically a very dubious attribution, to say the least), but remain silent on Aristotle's attempts to interpret human action in everyday life. Delineating psychology as a scientific discipline requires a fundamental abandonment of moral philosophy and ethics. In the following, we will encounter this same attitude in various philosophies of science. In the last sections we will see how hermeneuticians try to rehabilitate everyday understanding as a basis for interpretative discourse.

2. *Logical Positivism*

During the 1920's a new philosophy of science was formulated. A group of philosophers and scientists, calling themselves the "Vienna Circle", was inspired by the ideas of the positivist Comte, scientist Mach, the mathematician Russell, and the logician-philosopher Wittgenstein to propose a new criterion for a foundation of scientific knowledge. It was felt that a criterion was required to finally distinguish sensible knowledge from metaphysical nonsense. This criterion came to be known as the principle of verifiability: statements are meaningful only when their truth can be verified. This enables one to label metaphysical and theological propositions as meaningless: they could not be verified following logical analysis. An idea of an atomistic reality was presupposed, consisting of separate facts that could in principle be mapped by language or knowledge. This picture of language and reality has been beautifully sketched by Wittgenstein in his book, the *Tractatus Logico-Philosophicus* - a Bible for logical positivism, although there were some problems in interpreting the portions of the book that dealt with ethics.

Logical positivism originally believed in a world consisting of neutral, atomistic, separate facts, which can be known without presupposing a theoretical framework. Matters of fact can be described using a neutral observation language. Thus a certain unshakable basis is laid for the architecture of scientific theory. Inductive reasoning leads the scientist from singular to general statements. The combination of a certain basis and unshakable logical inferences leaves nothing to chance.[1]

As we shall see in section 7, the influence of different formulations of logical positivism on psychology has persisted up to the present. The demise of logical positivism in philosophy does not prevent psychologists from implicitly using the same principles in their research methods and in the construction of theories. In the Netherlands, the textbook by A.D. de Groot, *Methodology* (1961), has lend logical-empiricist ideas wide popularity in the social sciences. Despite this, it has been maintained that De Groot's methodology has a critical-rationalist character (see Hofstee 1985a, and De Vries 1984, 1986). In later sections we will encounter Gergen's arguments against what he calls the empiricist assumptions of the predominant school of social psychology. It seems that logical-positivist ideas, though modified into the weaker formulations of present-day logical empiricism (usually called the "received view of science"), are still present in reductionist methods for evaluating theories by recourse to simplistic experimental tests, and in the use of the concept of statistical significance (Bakan 1970; see section 7). It has been proposed to adopt a radical critical rationalist methodology in psychology in order to encourage audacious new hypotheses (Hofstee 1980, Koele 1979). The next section will deal with Popper's critical rationalism.

3. *Critical Rationalism*

The main reasons that lead present-day philosophers of science to reject logical positivism have been formulated clearly by Karl Popper in 1934. In Popper's view, (a) observation is theory-laden; (b) there is no way to reach certainty in scientific knowledge; (c) no such thing as a principle of induction exists, and (d) conclusive verification of general propositions like laws of nature is logically impossible. Scientific research starts with problems and devises theories or hypotheses to solve these problems. From the viewpoint offered by these theories, one is able to look for relevant observations and facts. Evaluation of theories with the help of basic propositions is possible, but basic propositions are theory-laden and have a provisional character. The scientific community has decided to accept them for the time being. According to Popper, reopening the discussion about the correctness or adequateness of basic propositions remains possible any time new observations are made or new theoretical considerations arise. Laws of nature, for instance, are valid for an infinite domain, extending to past and future cases, which makes it impossible to exclude the possibility of future falsification. Deduction is the only valid logical reasoning. The deduction of singular statements from general statements is valid, logically speaking; the inductive step in the reverse direction is not. The criterion of demarcation that Popper formulates concerns the scientific character of statements, not the question whether they are meaningful. A scientific hypothesis or theory must, in principle, be falsifiable. According to this criterion, metaphysics does not qualify as science, but it could provide useful ideas for the creation of hypotheses. This context of discovery, however, with its creative and intuitive aspects, is not a proper object for philosophy of science, according to Popper, but for the psychology of scientists. He is concerned with the logic of scientific discovery, that is, the logic of justification.

Some parts of Popper's philosophy are formulated so radically that they have found little support from other philosophers and have not been put to the test in scientific practice. The advice to formulate risky hypotheses and to aim for their falsification (instead of confirmation, which would encourage dogmatism and block progress) has never been received with enthusiasm. Psychologists, for instance, are interested in finding an answer to the question how humans function. Usually they are much too fond of the insights they possess to unrelentingly criticize their preliminary answers. Accordingly, experiments are frequently set up to confirm hypotheses or to accumulate new empirical evidence. If one does not succeed in this attempt, the research is generally regarded as a failure and journals are reluctant to publish such results. In other words, practice doesn't conform to Popperian standards which could give rise to doubts about their prescriptive and descriptive adequacy.

Of course, it could be argued that the tendency to avoid falsification described above is a typical characteristic of the field of psychology. Indeed, the latter has been the diagnosis of Hofstee (1980) who regards it as a weakness of psychological methodology that it allows such conservatism in research. Towards the other extreme of the methodological continuum we find Gergen (1982), who argues from a hermeneutical perspective that psychology must exploit its ability to confirm any empirical hypothesis as a creative possibility (see section 10). However, it is more probable that Popper's falsificationism has not been put into practice in any other part of science. Derksen has analyzed Popper's deductivism and come to the conclusion that Popper is not able to reject inductivism completely (1980, p. 157). This means that a strict falsificationism-deductivism is not even possible in an abstract sense.

It has been Popper's great merit to have questioned a number of empiricist assumptions very early. The importance he attaches to the development of theories emphasizes research as a human activity. On the other hand, he seems to be insensitive to the non-rational aspects of human knowledge. In the following sections we will see how Kuhn and Lakatos have tried to account for this. Popper is willing to grant the necessity of some dogmatism at the proper moment (1970, p. 55), but he is persistent in his rejection of the "myth of the framework". He maintains that frameworks may be criticized, changed, and replaced any time (1961; 1970, p. 56). This is questionable. Many philosophers have argued that human practices and rationality exist largely within frames of language and forms of life that remain unnoticed and unconscious most of the time; and even if some parts and aspects become an object for reflection it is doubtful whether they may be so easily changed, even if we would wish this. Such doubts have been formulated by Gadamer (1960) in his analysis of effective history and the small part played in it by historical consciousness; by Wittgenstein (1969) in his analysis of certainty and doubt; and by Kuhn (1962) in his description of normal science.

Finally, a few remarks have to be made on Popper's idea of the "logic of the situation". This concept invites our attention to the motives and reasons for acting in a particular situation. The rationality of human action depends on the specific logic required in a given situation. If we wish to understand why somebody acted as he did, we need to reconstruct the whole problem situation. This approach seems fruitful to me but difficult to reconcile with the idea that science aims to find deductive-nomological explanations. One could argue, in the line of Von Wright's *Explanation and Understanding* (1971), that the logic of the situation is a form of understanding with the benefit of hindsight. The practical syllogism involved leads to quasi causes, but not to deductive-nomological explanations; as Von Wright puts it at one point, "the behavior's intentionality is its *place* in a story about the agent" (1971, p. 115).

Popper, in all probability, would not easily go so far as Von Wright in casting doubt on deductive-nomological explanation as a model for the social sciences. Indeed, his criterion of demarcation, falsifiability, would have to be modified in the hypothetical case that not prediction and explanation, but understanding with hindsight would become a legitimate aim for the psychological sciences. It would necessitate him to revise his criticism of psychoanalysis as a pseudo-science (1963, p. 35; 1983, p. 163 ff) and to concede that all humanities are alike in this respect: part of their task consists of providing understanding of concrete cases with hindsight.[2] (This is not the same as giving explanations ad hoc). Psychologists in the empirical-analytical tradition have always been proud of having Popper on their side: with his arguments psychoanalysis could more easily be indicted as unscientific. In the past decades, however, more and more voices are heard, arguing for a far-reaching similarity between psychoanalysis and academic psychology in respect to their actual forms of research and theoretical status, e.g. Sharpe (1987). Their arguments will be discussed when we look at the hermeneutical perspective. First we have to look at some influential reactions to Popper from within the philosophy of natural science.

4. *Kuhn's Paradigms*

Kuhn is inspired by Popper's historical approach to science. He transforms it into a typical hermeneutical approach that takes the finite character of human experience into consideration. Whereas it seems obvious to Popper that there is progress after the overthrow of theories, Kuhn questions the nature of this progress. What are the criteria for measuring the rationality of progress? Usually they are formulated in terms of the latest theoretical framework. How valid is this framework? In Popper's terms it may be characterized as fallible. But then, is not every judgment on rationality and progress relative to a fallible framework? Popper has refrained from drawing this obvious conclusion from his own philosophy. Kuhn was the first to claim that there are no absolute criteria for truth, scientific knowledge, or rationality. And though he never equated science with arbitrariness or subjectivity, he has frequently been accused of being an irrationalist. This is a misunderstanding that may easily arise from a foundationalist position, and is surely an attack directed at the core of Kuhn's thought. Indeed, the most original contributions Kuhn has made to the philosophy of science are those where he points to the finitude of human knowledge. He has arrived at these ideas in the course of his work as a historian of the natural sciences. It dawned on him that the intellectual activity of the historian is vastly different from that of the scientist, and deserves its own status. He ended up as a hermeneutician rejecting the empirical-analytical imperialism which has been so influential in the social sciences (see section 7): "What has troubled me about the covering law model is that it makes of the historian a social scientist *manqué* . . . . It makes it hard to recognize that he has another and a profound discipline of his own, that there is an autonomy (and integrity) of historical understanding" (Kuhn 1977, p. 18).

The phases of development in science sketched by Kuhn are too well-known to need extensive recapitulation here. A field proceeds from an immature preparadigmatic phase into a period of paradigmatic science once agreement is reached concerning the proper way of study in nature. Typically, such agreement depends on the availability of convincing examples of research. Once such a "paradigm" has been created, metaphysical disputes on foundational and methodological issues come to an end, and scientists may proceed by trying to solve the "puzzles" left unsolved by the paradigm. This is called "normal science". After a certain period, the number of anomalies that arise becomes a threat for the paradigm, and the need for another paradigm will be felt. This state of crisis will lead to a revolution as soon as a new, convincing paradigm has been articulated. When certain conditions are fulfilled, a new period of normal science emerges. According to Kuhn, this cycle may be observed in the history of all branches of natural science.

The primary meaning of the concept "paradigm" is that of "examplar" of good scientific research (Kuhn 1962, p. 10; 1977, p. 298). According to Kuhn, scientific research resembles many other human activities in one crucial respect: it is not entirely rule-governed. To think that rules can account for everything results in an overevaluation of the rationality of research. Apart from this, what we may call epistemological argument, Kuhn claims that historical and sociological observations show that scientists are guided in their research by concrete scientific achievements called paradigms or examplars. Rules in themselves are never sufficient. They leave room for interpretation. Shared investigative practices are taught to students as a kind of initiation into the field and are presupposed in any explanation in theoretical terms.

An effect of the finite character of human experience is that scientific research is conducted within theoretical frameworks and according to paradigms that are "given" and not open to discussion. As a result, "normal science" deserves the epithet "dogmatic". According to Popper, such an attitude is uncritical and forms a danger to "critical" science as well as to society (Popper 1970, p. 53). Kuhn, on the contrary, is willing to accept the fact that rational thought is fundamentally bound to social *praxis*. Criticism, doubt, and puzzle-solving are possible thanks to dogmatism, certainty, and the acceptance of paradigms of research by scientists. It would be humanly impossible to expect that scientists pursue falsification of the existing paradigms all the time: it would only mean a waste of time, satisfy no one, and certainly not lead to progress of any kind. In Kuhn's vision, it is only in periods of normal science that there is unambiguous progress in puzzle-solving capacities. But we cannot objectively compare two paradigms and be sure there has been progress after a revolution, except on the basis provided by the new paradigm.

A hermeneutically interpreted history of science need not preclude the possibility of progress. The main problem lies in the historical point of view that threatens to relativize every judgment. Philosophy of science can adopt a Darwinian evolutionary perspective. In Kuhn's words, "the developmental process described in this essay has been a process of evolution *from* primitive beginnings - a process whose successive stages are characterized by an increasingly detailed and refined understanding of nature. But nothing that has been or will be said makes it a process of evolution *toward* anything" (1962, p. 170-1). Yet we are very accustomed to seeing science as a rational enterprise that draws us closer to some goal set in advance. In the present situation of serious environmental problems, caused in part by scientific and technological progress, it becomes easier to see the other side of the coin. Progress is seldom unambiguous. On an abstract theoretical level, it is often not difficult to point to phenomena left unexplained by the newest paradigm which could be explained by the older paradigm. But nobody cares or even notices them since the whole world view has changed, including criteria for sound knowledge (Kuhn 1977, p. 290). Every judgment on progress is bound to be complex and ambiguous: this is why Kuhn speaks of the incommensurability of paradigms. This concept does not imply -- as it is often understood-- that all comparison is meaningless and that we are left in utter relativism (see Kuhn 1962/1970, p. 206; 1977, Ch. 11).

On the reception of Kuhn's ideas in psychology we can be short. During the seventies, Kuhn has become one of the most quoted authors (cf. Peterson 1981). He is frequently used as support for the thesis that in psychology several mutually contradictory potential paradigms coexist alongside one another at the same time. Actually, Kuhn's remarks on the social sciences give the impression that he thinks they will remain preparadigmatic forever. The reason is that they lack the kind of puzzles which can be solved in relative isolation from everyday discourse. As Kuhn argues, "it is no criterion of goodness in a puzzle that its outcome be intrinsically interesting or important. On the contrary, the really pressing problems, e.g. a cure for cancer or the design of a lasting peace, are often no puzzles at all, largely because they may not have any solution" (1970, p. 36-7). Such problems possess a relevance that makes them worth studying, even if they defy a final solution.

Also, Kuhn is quoted as demonstrating that progress and rationality in the natural sciences are essentially contested concepts and that external factors play a role in the development of theories. This is taken as an excuse for what is sometimes called "the crisis in psychology": the never-ending philosophical debates about methods, foundations, and conceptual issues between different schools of psychoanalytical thought. For examples of such discussions, see Beijk & Roskam (1977) and recent issues of the *Newsletter for Uninomic Psychology*.

In conclusion, it seems that the lesson taught by Kuhn in psychology is not the same one that Kuhn intended to teach.[3] Where Kuhn points to fundamental differences between paradigmatic sciences and (still - or forever) preparadigmatic immature disciplines, psychologists have only noted that an extended use of the concept of paradigm, meaning something like "world view", could be applied to the plethora of schools of thought in psychology as well, and could legitimize them.

5. *Lakatos' Research Programs*

Imre Lakatos belonged to the Popperian school of critical rationalism. In response to Kuhn's criticism of falsificationism, he developed a more sophisticated form of falsificationism which is known as the "methodology of scientific research programs" (Lakatos 1970). According to Lakatos, it makes no sense to say that an isolated proposition is 'scientific'. Its meaning depends on the whole of a theoretical system. Neither can the predicate 'scientific' be applied to theories: this would require a kind of instant rationality, irrespective of the complexities of the development of science. Only the development of a theory undergoing continuous modifications may be called "(un-)scientific". This is what Lakatos calls a research program: a series of theories defined by a "hard core" of essential assumptions and a "protective belt" of statements that may be changed under the pressure of empirical evidence. Further, there is a "positive heuristic" consisting of guidelines on how to develop the theoretical ideas, and a "negative heuristic" stating how to protect the hard core and which directions are to be avoided. If a research program is able to find novel facts, one may speak of a "progressive problem shift", and such a program deserves the title "scientific". On the other hand, there are those programs which are hardly able to protect their hard cores, continuously making ad hoc modifications in the protective belt, without the regular appearance of novel predictions. In those cases, we should speak of a degenerating problem shift and withhold support for the program.

This is the essence of Lakatos' attempt to improve Popper's falsificationism. In many respects we are reminded of Kuhn's ideas. Lakatos claims explicitly that the choice between research programs is a rational affair, although it might take a long time to assess whether a research program leads to a progressive or a degenerating problem shift. Unfortunately, Lakatos isn't able to say how long we should give a degenerating program the benefit of the doubt.

Lakatos has accused Kuhn of irrationalism (1970, p. 93). Ironically, his own failure to provide clear criteria for progress and rationality in science has again drawn attention to the essentially contested nature of these concepts. His differences with Kuhn's acceptance of a certain form of dogmatism in normal science seems to be largely verbal. Paul Feyerabend has commented that "standards of this kind have practical force only if they are combined with a *time limit* . . . . Thus the standards which Lakatos wants to defend are either *vacuous*-- one does not know when to apply them -- or they can be criticized on grounds very similar to those which led to them in the first place. . . . one can [only] retain such standards as a *verbal ornament* . . ." (1970, p. 215). If one looks at Urbach's (1974) attempt to apply Lakatos' methodology to psychological research programs, one could draw the conclusion that the comparison between environmental and biological explanations of intelligence is a very complex affair, where a final judgment is not independent from value-laden assumptions on the matter. This would seem to lend support to Kuhn's thesis that each viewpoint is dependent on a theoretical framework. My own conclusion is that we are dealing here with a typical example of a conflict within the social sciences. We see a clash between philosophical and political convictions as much as a rational debate which can only be solved with reference to empirical evidence.

For the social sciences it certainly is important that Lakatos emphasizes the competition between several research programs. This could serve as a stimulus for critical discussions in contemporary psychology, often characterized by a lack of discussions and critical exchanges between several schools of thought that seem to remain unnecessarily isolated from each other.

6. *The Received View: Hempel's Model of Scientific Explanation*

The attention lavished on discussions between Popper, Kuhn, and Lakatos (and also philosophers not mentioned here, like Feyerabend,

Laudan, Toulmin, and Sneed) could easily give the impression that philosophy of science is itself preparadigmatic and can be broken down into competing Kuhnian and Popperian schools of thought. This is not the case. Apart from those who have moved away from philosophy of science proper, and practice science dynamics or sociology of science, there are numerous adherents of the so-called "received view", the logical empiricist conception of scientific theories that has evolved gradually out of logical positivism. Past supporters of the received view of science include logical empiricists like Carnap, Nagel, Suppe, Hempel, and Stegmüller, who were primarily interested in the structure of theories, the relations between observational and theoretical terms, the character of laws of nature and explanation, and problems connected to the notion of causality, to mention only a few examples. A.D. de Groot's *Methodology* is conceived in this tradition (see De Vries 1984, p. 47). Academic psychology has been much more influenced by the ideas of the Received View than by the philosophies of Popper and Kuhn put together: not only methodology in the strict sense, but also the self-conception of psychologists is impregnated by logical empiricism. In the present context, I will only say a few words about Hempel's model of scientific explanation. This model is known under a variety of names that basically refer to the same thing: the "HO-model" (from Hempel and his co-author Oppenheim), "hypothetico-deductive model", "deductive nomological explanation", the "covering-law model", or the "subsumption model".

According to Hempel, every scientific explanation ought to conform to the following characteristics. The phenomenon to be explained (the *explanandum*) is logically deduced from an *explanans* containing at least one law (sometimes statistical in nature) and usually a number of initial conditions. There must be some empirical evidence supporting the *explanans*. It must be true and the logical deduction must be valid (Hempel 1965, p. 331 ff). With probability laws in statistical explanations, the *explanandum* will only follow with a certain probability.

Hempel claimed that this model forms an explication of scientific explanation in all disciplines. Sometimes laws are simply omitted in explanations, but they are still presupposed. An example of such an elliptical explanation could be the following. I might try to explain why my colleague Willem Albert Wagenaar crosses the street in front of our office by saying: "He is going to have a drink in a nearby pub". Implicitly assumed is a law like: "fellows of the Psychological Institute who would like a drink usually cross the street to reach one of the pubs on the other side". The scheme of explanation would look like this:

- W.A. Wagenaar needs a drink
- W.A. Wagenaar is a fellow of the Psychological Institute
- Fellows of the Psychological Institute cross the street if they wish to get a drink *(explanans)*

- W.A. Wagenaar crosses the street (*explanandum*)

This is an example of a practical syllogism which conforms to the HO-model. It is interesting to note how much is left implicit, also in this artificial formulation: the person providing such an explanation and those for whom it is meant, seem to share an understanding of the situation (see MacNamara et al 1988 and Von Wright 1971).

Hempel's claim that the HO-model is presupposed in any valid scientific explanation has led to debates involving disciplines such as history and the social sciences. For instance, it has been argued by Dray (1957) that it is irrelevant for historical explanations whether the actors involved, or people in general, always or regularly act in a certain manner. According to Dray, what matters is the question whether it was *rational* to do a certain thing (cf. Ankersmit 1984). In the same spirit one could contend that a historical action or occurrence is only explained when we are able to weave a convincing and true narrative around it: this is what is called "narrative explanation".

In psychology there has been less resistance against Hempel's ideas. Roes (1985) has tried to demonstrate that laws exist in psychology and are used in explaining human behaviour. However, there are serious problems attached to this position. "Laws" in psychology are hardly similar to the laws of nature Hempel started out with. Leaving disciplines like the psychology of perception and psychophysiology out of consideration, "laws" in psychology not only have a statistical character -- that would in itself not really form a serious problem-- but they seem to be very context-bound and contingent. They lack the character of necessary truths that laws of nature typically possess; they are not ahistorical and they can rarely be explained by theories or higher-order laws. Psychological "laws" presuppose a social context that is historical and ever-changing, as Gergen (1982) and Billig (1987), among others, have demonstrated convincingly (see section 11). MacNamara et al (1988) argue that laws are not used in the explanation of actions. When we question the existence or the usefulness of laws in psychology, this is not the same as saying that we are not able to predict, or that knowledge concerning regularities is impossible. However, the manner in which psychologists deal with "expectations" is so different from the "predictions" used in the natural sciences, that it is very misleading to obscure the differences and pretend one is talking about the same thing. Understandably, deductive-nomological explanation has a high status: the natural sciences have booked impressive successes in prediction and technological control. This makes psychologists eager to imitate their methods, especially when renowned philosophers of science call upon them to do so.

7. *The Empirical-Analytical Method in Psychology*

The practice of psychological research is still dominated by an empiricist meta-theory. There are some who defend critical rationalism on the methodological level. But there is a growing minority who support several alternatives to the empirical-analytical approach.

Let me provide some examples of logical empiricist thought. In the Netherlands, A.D. de Groot's *Methodology* has been influential and forms a suitable case for treatment. The book has introduced American research principles into Dutch psychology:

1. Research is to be conducted according to an "empirical cycle". Tentative solutions to problems are formulated in the form of testable hypotheses. These lead to predictions. Predictions are tested in experiments or through systematic observation. "When I know something, I am able to predict; only when I am able to

predict, I know something" (1961, p. 92).

2. Results of empirical tests are evaluated statistically. If the null hypothesis (which one does not believe to be true, and which is not predicted) may be discarded, the hypothesis is regarded as confirmed: the probability of its truth is increased (p. 106).
3. The correctness of predictions may be verified; the truth of basic statements may be assessed objectively and with certainty (p. 96).
4. A distinction can be made between observational and theoretical statements.
5. The method for making predictions unambiguous is to operationalize concepts completely. In many cases this is possible without there being any surplus meaning: a concept is defined completely by a number of experimental variables (p. 89).

It has been argued by De Vries (1984, p. 47) that these assumptions form a clear case of logical empiricist thought. More important, these assumptions are still prevalent in present-day psychology. This means that Popper's influence must not be exaggerated. As regards (2), it must be noted that Bakan, Koele, and several others have argued for a more careful use of tests of significance with arguments drawn from critical rationalism. This has not resulted in any change in practice (Bakan 1970, Koele 1979, Tholey 1982, Fischhoff et al 1983). (1) makes clear that De Groot not only argues for the relative right of the empirical-analytical method, but defends an empirical-analytical world view. To him there is no knowledge other than predictive knowledge. In regard to (5), we have seen earlier how Popper argues that basic propositions are conventional and theory-laden. The majority of psychologists, we may safely say, still follow De Groot in his empiricist foundationalism. Readers believing that present-day methodological thought has far surpassed De Groot may be referred to research practices in social psychology, as analyzed by Cartwright (1973), Billig (1987), and Gergen (1982).

Van Strien (1986) points to several interpretative aspects present in the nomological approach. Research according to the empirical cycle is interlaced with decisions that can only be described as interpretations. A methodologist like De Groot is not blind to this, but he tries to exorcise the danger of subjectivism by stating that such interpretations will be tested in the course of the empirical cycle. Interpretations of empirical results of hypothesis testing may be tested in turn by again going through the phases of the cycle. Interpretations of closed sets of phenomena could be formulated as testable hypotheses with the help of some tricks, like partitions of the material (De Groot 1961, p. 326 ff). As I said earlier, this reduction of interpretations into empirical-analytical hypotheses is only possible given several logical-empiricist assumptions, like the availability of an objective certain basis. These assumptions are difficult to defend.

The way in which prominent representatives of modern philosophy of science assume science to be empirical-analytical science, restricts the validity of their conclusions. In chapter 5 I will argue against Adolf Grünbaum that the empirical-analytical method constitutes one of the possible approaches to reality. When Grünbaum criticizes psychoanalysis for the weaknesses inherent in its clinical evidence, in my opinion he adopts an empirical-analytical world view throughout his whole argument (see chapter 5). Hermeneutics and empirical-analytical science may be distinguished by their knowledge aims, instead of the object they try to explain. The humanities do not need a different method of research because their object isn't accessible to analysis or experimental research (as was claimed by Windelband in the idiographic-versus-nomothetic debate in the 19th century). Human reality may be studied by both empirical-analytical and empirical-hermeneutical methods. The dif-ference lies in what one wants to know. In the next section I will discuss hermeneutical approaches, beginning with Gadamer's philosophical hermeneutics and continuing with some applications of his thought to psychology.

8. *Hermeneutics: Philosophical Reflection on Interpretation*

Let me start with a positive and relatively simple definition: hermeneutics means the philosophical reflection on the practice of interpretation, whereby phenomena are understood as dependent parts of larger contexts. Hermeneutic philosophers stress the fact that interpretation is not restricted to science but starts with everyday life. But it must be emphasized that hermeneutics has long since abandoned obscure notions of "Verstehen" and emphatic understanding by means of "Einfühlen" or reenactment. Hermeneutics in psychology is often equated with subjective acts of intuitive "Verstehen" (see Van Strien 1986, Sanders & Van Rappard 1987), but such notions are explicitly rejected by Gadamer (1960) and modern authors whose aim is to introduce hermeneutical method in psychology and the social sciences, like Abel (1975), Hekman (1984), or Messer, Sass & Woolfolk (1988).

In this respect, there is a great similarity between modern hermeneutics and the later philosophy of Wittgenstein. Analyzing the notion of intentionality, Wittgenstein concluded that the meaning of actions and expressions is not to be found in inner subjective occurrences, but lies in the rules that are followed. We understand an action if we are familiar with the language game it belongs to; if not, we form hypotheses about the rules followed and the language game being played. In the end, understanding human beings depends on a familiarity with forms of life: "if a lion could talk, we could not understand him" (1953, p. 223), because "to imagine a language means to imagine a form of life" (par. 19). Wittgenstein is not denying that we have feelings and intentions, but he points to the context in which such concepts are used and get their meaning. "Only of a living human being and what resembles (behaves like) a living human being can one say: it has sensations; it sees; is blind; hears; is deaf; is conscious or unconscious" (1953, par. 281).

Likewise, hermeneutics assumes that understanding is a fundamental human possibility which is initially displayed in the prescientific every-day world. Secondarily, it may be practiced systematically in a scientific context. I have distinguished several characteristics of hermeneutical understanding elsewhere (see Chapter 6) which can be summarized in the following points:

a. *The hermeneutical circle.* Interpretation begins with a preconception about the object (text, culture, language game). Reading a book, for instance, we have a rough expectation about the whole if we start with the first sentences. The details are understood from the whole, but the whole is understood, in turn, from an understanding of the parts. We may move forward and backward,without ever leaving this circle or cycle.

b. *Internal relations.* The interpreter looks for meaning relations between, e.g. words, actions, or expressions as they are found in a given context, and defined by the rules of the language game in question.

c. *Individual cases.* Understanding is directed at puzzling concrete phenomena as they are found. Understanding may be generalized, but this isn't essential. In this sense, idiographic insight is sufficient.

d. *Fusion of horizons.* Hermeneuticians assume a distance between the subject (interpreter) and the object (to be interpreted). This distance is put into the metaphor that the horizons of understanding diverge. A complete understanding may aim for a fusion of horizons, in Gadamer's terminology.

e. *Application.* Any understanding of historical phenomena is an attempt to apply its meaning in the present. Trying to understand a classic text means assuming that it has something to say, that it still claims to be true. The task for the interpreter is to bring out this truth in an application to the present situation. Or if the distance is not one in time but in culture, the problem is what another culture may have to tell us, instead of assuming that our own culture is superior. The interpreter should bring his own preconceptions into the open: interpretation looks like a dialogue between two parties.

With these brief examples, I hope it has become clear what the differences are between hermeneutics and the empirical-analytical approach to reality.

9. *The Hermeneutical Approach in Psychology*

Hermeneutics consists of philosophical reflection on practices of interpretation. Psychology is one such practice - in many varieties: psychotherapy, social psychology, dream interpretation, etc. - and there are several schools of thought proposing interpretative methods. Most of them view interpretative approaches as alternatives to the traditional empirical-analytical method. Usually it is contended that a differential approach may lead to an adequate method for each field of psychology. Donald Taylor (1987), for example, opposes the "doctrine of hermeneutics" to the "doctrine of mechanism" and argues that the first doctrine is more adequate in the study of accidents and safety behavior. Van Strien (1986) demonstrates how traditional empirical-analytical methodology is unable to guide the practitioner in psychology. In his view, there is a complementary relation between hermeneutics and the empirical cycle of research. In practical situations it is difficult to apply knowledge of nomological relations. Concrete cases are not understood by subsumption under laws. The practitioner uses a "regulative cycle" consisting of the following steps: problem - diagnosis - plan - intervention - evaluation. Such "practical thought" is directed at individual, instead of general knowledge; it leads to interventions, not to statements, and it is directed by norms and values.

Similar arguments have been brought forward in other fields. Runyan (1982) has argued for the use of interpretative approaches in psychohistory. He emphasizes the fact that interpretations can be empirically evaluated; even if several interpretations are possible, we may be able to rule out arbitrariness. Erdelyi (1985) has analyzed psychoanalytic interpretations from the vantage-point of cognitive psychology. From his analysis, it emerges that we cannot avoid interpretation, neither in daily life nor in psychology, and that we are in many cases amply justified in drawing conclusions concerning the meaning of our experiences and observations.

For hermeneuticians, the way psychologists deal with their object is structurally similar to the way we deal with people in everyday life. Psychologists use practical knowledge, reminiscent of Aristotle's prudence (phronesis), and not technical insights. Like Aristotle, they don't expect the exactness and precision in human affairs that are reached in the natural sciences. But that should not lead us to think that practical knowledge is only arbitrary and subjective.

10. *The Rhetorical Approach in Psychology*

More radical than Van Strien's use of hermeneutics is the approach advocated by rhetorical psychology. As we have seen in the previous section, Van Strien c.s. views the interpretative and empirical-analytical methods as complementary. If used in the proper context, empirical-analytical research is accepted without further reservations. We could, however, inquire into the interpretative or rhetorical aspects of traditional empiricist research, assuming that all knowledge in the humanities rests on interpretative assumptions - though these are normally hidden and implicit. Speaking in this vein, Donald McCloskey (1983) has analyzed modern economical theory as a rhetorical enterprise. The difference with Van Strien is that McCloskey does not propose an alternative method: he suggests that economists should reflect on what they are actually doing in their research and realize what the assumptions of their theories are.

Rhetoricians like Michael Billig and Kenneth Gergen claim that the entire empirical-analytical approach rests on implicit interpretations. First of all, they point out that traditional empirical-analytical research in (social) psychology is historically bound. Exact quantitative hypothesis testing is an activity taking place within a cultural framework, consisting of norms, values, and prescientific assumptions. Looking back on research from twenty or thirty years ago, we recognize these values and the relativity of the hypotheses found at that time because our society has changed (and in connection with that, the theoretical framework from which we evaluate as well). Examples of the historically-determined character of empirical-analytical research in psychology are provided by Gergen (1973; 1982, ch. 1), Morawski & Goldstein (1985), Samelson (1980), and Billig (1987).

Such demonstrations of the relativity of psychological research do not imply that it is senseless to search for laws and to test hypotheses. They only make clear that empirical-analytical research has no privileged access to an ahistorical basis of brute facts that are neutral in regard to societal values. As Duintjer (1970) puts it, empirical-analytical science may try to avoid values in the descriptive language about the object (according to the ideal of being value-free in the Weberian sense), but it remains necessarily committed to values in the foundations of research.

These values cannot be avoided, but they could be made explicit. An example is formed by the values that guide the choice of selective viewpoints, research questions, and conceptual frameworks within scientific theories. At least in the humanities, the choice of a theoretical framework is never guided by purely internal theoretical considerations. Non-theoretical external factors exert their influence in opaque ways that are frequently unknown to the investigators.

Apart from the historical and cultural dimension of psychological knowledge, Gergen has shown the importance of interpretations and values at various levels of empirical-analytical research. The identification of actions poses a multitude of possibilities, to be restrained only by contingent social conventions and variable contextual indicators (Gergen 1980; 1982, ch. 2). The fact that we are usually able to understand what other people say and do in daily life depends on our familiarity with daily situations in which we find ourselves. Psychological experiments tend to eliminate this familiar context, thus causing actions, expressions, and utterances to be interpreted in various ways. Also, quite often certain interpretations are inadvertently suggested by the experimenter. A whole literature on "demand characteristics" and "experimenter effects" is devoted to these problems. On the other hand, psychological theories are applicable to reality in various ways. A psychological statement is only connected with practices of intervention and action by means of interpretations. Interpretations of actions are the rules of correspondence between theory and practice. This means that the truth of psychological theories is completely dependent, according to Gergen, on the creativity of those who invent these correspondence rules. There is no reason why we should leave this task to the investigators or those proposing a theory. Either the theory should prescribe explicitly how its theoretical statements are to be connected to observations and operationalizations, or these should speak for themselves. And surely they do speak for themselves, though in unexpected ways. Gergen has shown in several experiments that students are very creative in lending significance to any given psychological statement (1980, p. 249; Gergen et al 1986). Gergen's position is interesting because he doesn't conclude, from his hermeneutical meta-theory, that experimental research should be abandoned because of its ambiguity. In his view, empirical-analytical research forms a legitimate and useful possibility even if we have replaced traditional empiricist meta-theory by a hermeneutical alternative. He would only argue that usually the full implications of experimental research are left unexplored. He proposes looking at the results of empirical-analytical research with a different eye: we may see examples of interpretative possibilities instead of objective descriptions. When we abandon the empiricist assumption that there is a fixed reality that can be described objectively, the aims of scientific research must be redefined. Traditionally, science is supposed to provide true descriptions and explanations of reality, to predict phenomena, and to enable the control of these phenomena.

Gergen proposes different aims. In his proposal, psychology should furnish fresh alternatives for social action and challenge common-sense interpretation. Exploring new ways to view reality, an alteration of consciousness, challenging conventional interpretations, and furnishing fresh alternatives for social action are what Gergen calls "generative theorizing" (1982, Ch. 3; see chapter 4 of this volume for a more detailed exposition).

Let me conclude this short recapitulation of Gergen's ideas with some comments. In his continuous discussion of the dominant empiricist thought in psychology, Gergen is frequently tempted to defend provocative opposite positions.

Ironically, in his countertheses he sometimes uses the same assumptions as his empiricist opponents. To give an example, it could be argued that the openness and arbitrariness of interpretations is, in the first place, an artefact of context-poor social psychological experiments.[4] The characteristics of interpretations within this context cannot be generalized to interpretations in daily life or history. Also, the *possibility* of alternative interpretations provides insufficient grounds for concluding that our conventional interpretations are not alright as they are. As long as we are contented with our conventions, there is nothing wrong. In chapter 4, I will argue from a

Wittgensteinian point of view that Gergen neglects the cultural imbeddedness of a large part of our interpretative repertoire. In the same spirit, Jahoda (1986) has questioned Gergen's emphasis on human freedom. Indeed, in many cases we reach intersubjectivity in interpretation, both in daily life and in intellectual affairs, and we would be in serious trouble if this were not the case. On the other hand, we must admit that the basis of our interpretations is not rational; they are based on what I called earlier, using a Wittgensteinian concept, our forms of life. In his conceptions of freedom and human finitude, Gergen is vastly different from a hermeneutician like Gadamer who points out the impossibility of radical reflection on our historical situation. "The self-awareness of the individual is only a flickering in the closed circuits of historical life" (Gadamer 1960, p. 261; 1979, p. 245).

Like Billig (1987), Gergen is more interested in the ways interpretations are defended by means of persuasion, distorting the object and offering ever-changing visions of reality, than in the traditional meanings contained in our culture. The former are the traditional concerns of rhetorical philosophy. The Greek rhetoricians claimed against Plato that there is not a world of unchanging ideas behind the visible and changing phenomena, and that truth is constituted in persuasive discourses on reality. Language and reality cannot be separated and treated as two distinct entitities. Likewise, Michael Billig (1987) wants to show that the truths that psychologists try to sell are dependent on the language they use, their examples, the audience they try to reach, and their arguments. Truth is always two-sided. What psychologists claim to know, according to Billig, is usually not untrue, but partially true: in a different context, one could plausibly argue for exactly the opposite statement. The claim for the existence of universal social-psychological laws may safely be put aside if we carefully examine the history of psychology in this century. Laws, interpretations, theories, and arguments may not only be contested in the abstract: one can easily find examples of countertheses for any thesis ever formulated in psychology.

Thus Billig is close to Gergen in his evaluation of empirical-analytical psychology: both authors prefer ambiguity to objectivity and conformism, and paradoxes to logical precision.

11. *Concluding Remarks on the Status of Psychology: Preparadigmatic Science Forever, or on its Way to a Paradigm?*

What has been said so far gives us an opportunity to comment on what has been called the 'crisis' in psychology, and on a solution proposed for this alleged crisis, i.e., that psychologists should aim more persistently for unity in their discipline. Joseph R. Royce, in a paper read at the First Banff Conference on Theoretical Psychology in 1965, put it in these words: "complete unification in any discipline of study, such as physics or psychology, is impossible to attain, although it's a goal we should seek" (Royce 1970, p. 50). As we have seen in our discussion of Kuhn's ideas on preparadigmatic disciplines (see section 5), there are grounds to doubt whether physics and psychology should be grouped together in this respect. Psychologist Arthur W. Staats adopts the Kuhnian notion of psychology as a preparadigmatic science when he writes about "Psychology's Crisis of Disunity" and contends that "while psychology is a science in its many characteristics, it has not begun to attain the paradigmatic level of development" (Staats 1983, p. 141). For Staats it is clear that this description, though correct, is a bitter pill for psychologists to swallow, and he doesn't hesitate to formulate the aim of "uninomic psychology".

From a hermeneutical point of view we may well ask: (a) is this a realistic aim?; (b) is it worth pursuing?; and finally (c) is the diagnosis of a "crisis" justified and do we really have to worry about psychology as it is at the moment? These are the questions I'd like to answer briefly in this concluding section: no; not at any costs; and: no, only logical empiricists ought to worry, or perhaps they'd better change their philosophy of science.

The aim of unification in psychology seems to be based on the assumption that psychology is, in the relevant aspects, similar to the natural sciences. For some reason - maybe the subject matter is more complex, or psychology still lacks its 'Newton' -- it is still immature. I regard this as a very implausible view of the problems. The best arguments against it have been given by Thomas Kuhn, and I shall present these arguments with a little amplification from the vantage-point of hermeneutics.

Kuhn considers puzzle-solving to be an essential ingredient of normal science and he maintains that such puzzle-solving is only possible in a state of relative insulation. Scientists try to solve the puzzles considered to be most significant by their paradigm community, not by the general public. Now consider the difference between this and the situation in the social sciences. The problems encountered by these disciplines are often called relevant, and rightly so. Attempts at insulation are usually distrusted, and rightly so: insulation of a field and its language would form a threat for the relevance of the solutions offered. But this means, as quoted from Kuhn in an earlier section, that "the really pressing problems, e.g., a cure for cancer or the design of a lasting peace, are often not puzzles at all, largely because they may not have any solution. Consider the jigsaw puzzle whose pieces are selected at random from each of two different puzzle boxes" (Kuhn 1962, p. 37). In contrast, a scientific community acquires with a paradigm a criterion for choosing problems that, while the paradigm is taken for granted, can be assumed to have solutions. "A paradigm can, for that matter, even insulate the community from those socially important problems that are not reducible to the puzzle form . . . . such problems can be a distraction, a lesson brilliantly illustrated . . . by some of the contemporary social sciences" (ibid).

I think the notion of insulation helps to provide a good explanation for the problem why the social sciences are so different from the natural sciences. A psychologist might put the question like this: "Why does my field fail to move ahead in the way that, say, physics does? What changes in technique or method or ideology would enable it to do so?" (Kuhn 1962, p. 160).

The answer is that psychologists work to help and understand an audience of non-professionals: clients, patients, the general public, schoolteachers, or judges in court.[5] They have to speak two languages and be able to translate their professional concepts into everyday discourse. Insulation is an impossible ideal for most subdisciplines of psychology -- with the possible exception of certain technical subfields.

Psychology cannot aim to become an empirical science on the model of physics if this would require insulation. A revealing case is that of behaviorism, a theory with a strict empiricist approach which has frequently been described as a flight into sterility and abstract jargon, and the study of irrelevant problems. In many cases, this has led to insulation in the negative sense of the word, not even accompanied by much internal progress.

Therefore, looking at the multitude of conflicting theories and systems in the field of psychology, I certainly agree with Staats and other uninomic psychologists in their diagnosis that there is a problem in the tendency found in many schools of psychology to confine themselves to their own narrow theoretical frameworks, and avoid communication and critical discussions with others. We may agree on the idea that isolationism, or a disinterested relativistic attitude in the sense of "you may have your paradigm, if you let me keep mine", doesn't lead to progress or fresh insights in any field. As we have seen in section 8, Kuhn cannot be interpreted in this way. Theoretical differences in psychology are not simply "paradigm clashes" where communication is unnecessary or impossible. A psychological theory should not be insulated, neither from everyday discourse nor from a broader general discussion between various schools within the field. Where I disagree with Staats is in his idea of a "uninomic" theory as a remedy for disunity. It will be clear from what I have said before that I do not believe in the possibility of one set of integrated laws in this field -- which seems to be implied by the mongrel term 'uninomic'. But even if it would be possible, it would probably imply a degree of insulation unprecedented in the field. In view of this, my suggestion is to let the idea of unification remain as it is: a chimera of empiricists.

As to the last question, whether it is justified to speak of a crisis in psychology, the answer depends entirely upon what one expects. Those committed to an empiricist picture of science would expect steady accumulation of knowledge, the possibility of empirical evaluation of theories, a gradual vanishing of ambiguity and uncertainty, and consequently the unity of psychology as a science. The fact that this unity has not come about after a century of psychology as an empirical science must lead us to reflect on the adequateness of the empiricist assumptions. Though I sympathize with the honesty of Staats' diagnosis of the problems of disunity, I think his search for a solution is misguided because he stays within the confines of empiricism.[6]

For those who look upon the matter from a hermeneutical perspective, the problem is entirely different or non-existing. Hermeneuticians don't expect unity. They are familiar with the never-ending debates on the basic questions of philosophy, they will point out the rhetorical nature of human reality, and keep faith in the rational character of the enterprise as long as a dialogue remains possible. I hope it has become clear from the last section that this is not an attempt to obscure the fundamental problems of psychology, but a possibility to solve the problems by viewing the world differently. This is how Wittgenstein looked upon the matter some 40 years ago: "The confusion and barrenness of psychology is not to be explained by calling it a 'young science'; its state is not comparable with that of physics, for instance, in its beginnings . . . . For in psychology there are experimental methods and *conceptual confusion* . . . . The existence of the experimental method makes us think we have the means of solving the problems which trouble us; though problem and method pass one another by" (1953, II, xiv). This means that for Wittgenstein, the foundations of psychology pose philosophical problems of the form "I don't know my way about" (par. 123). And for their solution he only gave hints like this (par. 109): "The problems are solved, not by giving new information, but by arranging what we have always known. Philosophy is a battle against the bewitchment of our intelligence by means of language".

2

THE EARLY RECEPTION OF PSYCHOANALYSIS: VICISSITUDES OF A SCIENCE OF INTERPRETATION

> Psychoanalysis derives nothing but disadvantages from its middle position between medicine and psychology.
>
> Sigmund Freud

Contents:

1. *Introduction*

Freud's own view on the reception of his ideas has always been that they were received in an atmosphere of hostility. Psychoanalysis was either ignored or rejected. After a period of splendid isolation, from 1904 on he recruited a small but growing group of followers who formed his only point of security in a hostile world. Later they were to form the psychoanalytic movement. Freud tended to think of late nineteenth century Sexual Morality and antisemitism as the main causes of the rejection of psychoanalysis by the medical world and the lay public. Ernest Jones, his disciple and influential biographer, did little to correct this picture of the birth and early development of psychoanalysis.

We know better today. Historical research (Decker 1977, Sulloway 1979) has created a more complex view of the early reception of psychoanalysis. The psychiatric world was not so uniformly hostile as Freud and Jones liked to suggest. Freud had the illogical expectation that the entire medical world would immediately recognize the truths he offered, without paying attention to the more problematic assumptions he had made. Indeed, a fair amount of criticism was leveled against early psychoanalysis.

In this chapter, I will not enter the discussion of the balance between the number of uncomprehending reactions and the number of positive evaluations of psychoanalysis. My concern is with the nature of the critical remarks made by members of the psychiatric establishment and intellectuals capable of understanding what was going on, without being members of the psychoanalytic movement. Strictly speaking, this last comment is unnecessary, since it was impossible to be both an analyst and have critical ideas on psychoanalysis both at the same time.

Criticism had to come from outsiders. But outsiders could not be trusted as such, the argument being that if they would be capable of the least understanding of psychoanalysis, they would be psychoanalysts themselves. As an example, let me refer to some articles written by the German psychiatrists Aschaffenburg (1906) and Hoche (1910). Ernest Jones has nothing good to say about these opponents (1955, p. 124) and if we believe him, their articles contained nothing but vigorous attacks, moral indignation, and deep misunderstandings of psychoanalysis. Anyone who takes the trouble to read Aschaffenburg though, will see that his paper consists of perfectly reasonable arguments and objections, and is by no means radically opposed to psychoanalysis or Freud personally. Jung, who wrote a reply to Aschaffenburg when he was still a zealous disciple of Freud (Jung 1906), characterized "the attack" as 'very moderate and careful criticism'. There is one point in these articles which is especially interesting in the present context: both Hoche and Aschaffenburg speak of Freud's "art of interpretation" (*Deutekunst*) which shows the marks of genius but is also frequently arbitrary. They doubt that his explanations form the only possibilities of interpretation.

I will start from this very assumption. One might call it, hermeneutically speaking, a preconception (*Vorurteil)*, that is to say, that psychoanalysis is an interpretative discipline, aiming at understanding meaning in human life. This hermeneutical conception of psychoanalysis has become common among philosophers and analysts during the past decades.[1] There is a continuing discussion between the hermeneutical conception and the traditional self-understanding of psychoanalysis which holds that it is an empirical-analytical science, capable of providing deductive-nomological explanations (see chapter 5).

Now it is interesting to see that this modern discussion is foreshadowed by several reactions towards Freud's work given during his lifetime. These reactions could not lead to actual debates, however, because of the closed nature of the psychoanalytic movement at the time and the immunization strategies used by Freud and his followers. Let us first examine to the reactions Freud received from his psychiatric colleagues.

2. *Freud's reception in psychiatry*

Ernest Jones has provided an overview of the opposition which the psychoanalytical movement had to endure in the years before World War I (Jones 1955, ch. 4). He indicates a great difficulty in describing this opposition: a large part of it could not find its way into print, it was "simply unprintable". Without denying the existence and extent of miscellaneous non-scientific resistances against psychoanalysis, I will restrict myself here to the scientific literature in medical, psychiatric, and psychological journals. I hope to show that the nature of the criticism in these journals was not adequately understood by Jones or Freud. Precisely the ambiguous hermeneutical nature of psychoanalysis, if one wishes to use modern terminology, turns out to be a central feature in the criticism. I will refer to seven of the most interesting papers which aimed at evaluating Freud's work. Each of them is mentioned by Jones in the chapter referred to earlier. The authors are remarkably unanimous in their opinions regarding which parts of Freud's theory are valuable and which are not. Almost all of them provide informative surveys of Freud's already complex ideas.[2] Their aim is to evaluate these ideas using reasonable criteria, usually drawn from medical science and sometimes from philosophy.[3] Aschaffenburg (1906) and Hoche (1910) are the most polemical critics. As psychiatrists, they wish to make a stand against psychoanalysis, without feeling the need to descend to ad hominem attacks.[4] Several authors make a sharp distinction between the writings of Freud and those of his followers.[5] The followers are regarded as mere believers, members of a sect, who have no original contribution to make themselves. Their attitudes are rejected as being arrogant and ridiculous. Quite the contrary, Freud is esteemed highly and in between various criticisms his qualities and his valuable ideas are made explicit.[6] It would be hard to point out any signs suggesting antisemitism or a puritan sexual morality.[7] Talking to young girls about intimate sexual matters is not regarded as a matter of good taste, nor is it considered necessary. But there is no real reason against it if it were necessary for an effective therapy, as Aschaffenburg puts it.[8] Having summed up these more general issues, I can now turn to the main target of the criticism.

Most authors make it clear that the main point of disagreement lies in the interpretations Freud gives of symptoms, dreams, and behavior. The interpretations of the disciples are considered ridiculous and not worth serious attention.[9] Both the arbitrariness of single interpretations and the method of interpretation give rise to scepticism. Kronfeld is the most lucid critic of Freud's method of interpretation (1911, p. 235-248).[10] Free association may help a doctor to deepen his understanding of a patient's personality, but it could lead to any interpretation. Where should one stop the chain of associations? Could not any interpretation be confirmed when the doctor can make his choice from a multitude of associations? Is the choice of an interpretation not ultimately dependent upon the individual doctor? Does Freud not come up with very wild interpretations sometimes, without the least evidence that they might or must be true? Most authors answer these questions in the affirmative.[11] It is interesting to see that several authors acknowledge both positive and negative aspects in the work of interpretation. In their view, a positive aspect is the attention given to the psychological life of patients, to the individual biography, resulting in idiographic knowledge.[12] Freud's view that his interpretations are explanations or etiological causal relations is regarded as untenable. Freud suggests that his interpretations are scientific because they are backed by a reconstruction of the etiology of symptoms. This argument is shown to be circular.[13]

The second main controversial point is the universal character of sexuality. Both the change of meaning in the concept, as well as the idea that interpretations have to refer to sexual wishes, is regarded as speculative.[14]

What may be concluded from this overview? First, the articles reviewed corroborate the thesis brought forward by Decker (1977) and Sulloway (1979), that Freud's reception was much less hostile than Jones suggested.[15]

Second, no evidence is found for the belief that psychoanalysis was not accepted because of non-scientific or unreasonable motives such as those mentioned by Freud (1925e) and Jones (1955, Ch. 4).

Third, the actual reasons for the rejection of psychoanalysis as a full-fledged scientific discipline are different from what is generally believed. Freud is criticized for his particular method of interpretation, and for the arbitrariness of many of his interpretations, but not for his interpretative work in itself. I disagree with Decker when she says that the "ultimate rejection" of psychoanalysis had to do with "the failure of most German doctors to understand" it (1971, p. 481). The articles quoted are thorough evaluations of psychoanalysis and contain no major misunderstandings as seen from a present-day point of view.[16]

In conclusion it seems that the psychiatric community recognized the importance of Freud's work in the years before 1914. His theories were seen as important contributions to the understanding of individual psychological factors in connection with neurosis. The bone of contention was the status of these insights. Freud tried to sell them as scientific explanations which could provide insight into the etiology of symptoms. The scientific forum could not accept this idea.

Why was Freud so uncompromising in defending his new theory as a natural science? Apparently he didn't believe that a merely interpretative discipline would be treated with respect within medical science. His own philosophical thinking was based on a firm distinction between the methods of the natural sciences and the humanities (*Geisteswissenschaften*). Though the latter could be relevant for psychoanalysis, they used entirely different methods than those created by Freud, who was proud that he developed his insights from careful observation. To him, the latter claim could only be made by a natural scientist. According to Freud, his discoveries meant a revolution within medicine, without questioning the methodological foundations of the discipline. Let us try to elucidate the nature of the Freudian revolution by distinguishing between four different claims made by Freud.

(a) Psychological phenomena form a legitimate object for scientific study.
(b) There are unconscious psychological phenomena.
(c) Studying the unconscious of an individual is only possible by interpreting speech, action, dreams, symptoms, etc.
(d) The techniques of interpretation guarantee objective scientific results.

Freud's view, as described in *The Resistances to Psychoanalysis*, was that the psychiatric forum could not accept (a) and (b) because of the revolutionary nature of these assumptions. "They [the contemporary generation of physicians] had been brought up to respect only anatomical, physical, and chemical factors. They were not prepared for taking psychical ones into account and therefore met them with indifference and antipathy. They obviously had doubts whether psychical events allowed any exact scientific treatment whatever" (1925e, p. 215).

I hope that the above survey has shown that this explanation is not supported by existing evidence. Psychiatrists and philosophers were ready to accept the premises (a) and (b), although they were regarded as new and revolutionary. They were even prepared to accept the necessity of interpretation (c) but remained sceptical about the scientific character and objectivity of the interpretations given and the techniques used, point (d). Freud could not provide satisfying

answers to the questions raised about these matters. He evaded discussion by explaining criticisms as 'resistances'. This attitude towards legitimate critical questions directed at his theory was enthusiastically imitated by his followers, and may be the main cause of much irritation in scientific quarters. Opponents rightly felt that there was not much point in discussing matters with psychoanalysts. The psychoanalytic framework developed in isolation.
Let us see now whether the critical points raised so far found any resonance outside the field of psychiatry.

3. *Criticisms: Karl Kraus, Karl Popper, Arthur Schnitzler*

The journalist and critic Karl Kraus (1874-1936) seems to stand in the shadow of many of his better known fellow citizens. But it has frequently been pointed out how he exerted an enormous influence, in his time, through his lectures and his journal *Die Fackel*.[17] He embodied the moral ideals of many intellectuals, among them Wittgenstein and Popper, and up to a certain time, Freud. For some time, Kraus was sympathetic to Freud.[18] When followers of Freud started psychoanalyzing living artists, however, Kraus grew suspicious of psychoanalysis, and the final break was caused by Fritz Wittels when he tried to analyze the "Fackel-Neurosis" in a meeting of the Vienna Psychoanalytic Society in 1910. Kraus was enraged when he came to hear about this lecture, and *Die Fackel* was filled with biting aphorisms on psychoanalysis.[19]

In the present context, we can attempt to understand Kraus' reaction as follows. Kraus rejected the use which was made of psychoanalysis as an instrument for persuasion under the cover of objective neutral science. To him, this meant an unpermissible confusion between moral and scientific discourse. By presenting psychoanalysis as a scientific method, every interpretation made by an analyst gained a pseudo-objectivity which made it look superior to all other possible interpretations. Psychoanalysis, as a method of interpretation, sought to deny its own subjective nature by postulating a determinism of free associations and law-governed instincts. Human reality seemed to be reducible to natural processes by way of objective analysis.

A sample of Kraus' aphorisms will illustrate his ideas. "God made man out of dust. The analyst reduces him to it" (Szasz 1977, p. 105). "Psychoanalysis is a passion, not a science. It lacks the steady hand of the investigator . . . Psychoanalysis is, in fact, an act of revenge through which the analyst's inferiority is transformed into superiority . . . There is only one justification for the existence of psychoanalysis: it is useful for unmasking psychoanalysis" (Szasz, p. 106; Stekel, 1913, p. 641). "Psychoanalysis is the mental illness, for which it claims to be the cure", was Kraus' much-quoted conclusion. I will not go into the question whether this criticism concerns the uses made of psychoanalytic method, or whether it pertains to the essence of psychoanalytic theory. If one reads psychoanalytic 'explanations' of artists made at the time, one can scarcely avoid the conclusion that the arrogance and feelings of superiority in the first generation of analysts were rightly attacked by Kraus.

Much the same criticism was formulated by Karl Popper in a lecture delivered in 1953.[20] He explains how he came to his new criterion of demarcation between science and pseudo-science in 1919, though he never published about psychoanalysis as an example of pseudo-science at that time. The problem took the simple form, "what is wrong with Marxism, psychoanalysis, and (Adlerian) individual psychology"? (Popper 1963, p. 34). The answer is also surprisingly simple. Freud and Adler are dealt with in half a page. The mistake of Freudian analysts was to trust in the verification of their theories by "clinical observations". Instead, they should have been on the lookout for falsifications, according to Popper (ibid, p. 35). Apparently, Popper criticizes the uncritical attitude of analysts, but it is implied that there is something wrong with their theories which seem to consist of dubious techniques of interpretation designed to evade falsification. Freud is not quoted, nor are any of his theories mentioned in particular.

I am not concerned with the adequacy of this criticism here. Adolf Grünbaum (1984) has presented a convincing rebuttal of Popper's views.[21] Important in the present context is their enormous influence, which must be ascribed, in my opinion, to their partial truth. As shown earlier, the analytic community (later on, several communities) had a strong tendency to protect itself against criticism from outside. This was one reason why psychoanalysis was not accepted in scientific circles. Another reason was the Freudian art of interpretation which disturbed many colleagues, as we have seen. This is Popper's main point of criticism. Interpretations in terms of (unconscious) motives may be carefully made on the basis of reliable observations and other evidence, but still, speaking from a deductive-nomological point of view, they only provide ad hoc explanations. Possibilities of prediction are almost non-existent.

We can conclude that Popper hit a weak spot in psychoanalysis. He could avail himself of strict deductive-nomological standards because Freud regarded his theory as a natural science, but seen from that very point of view, it foundered.

Arthur Schnitzler (1862-1931) was trained as a medical doctor, but turned to a literary career early in his life. His interest in psychoanalysis began in the days of his medical practice when he was experimenting with hypnosis. A number of his aphorisms on psychoanalysis, stemming from the period 1904-26, were published in 1976. Freud felt that Schnitzler and he shared many insights in human motivation, and he spoke of Schnitzler as his Doppelgänger. In Bolkosky's words, "If Freud practiced psychoanalysis as an art, it was Schnitzler who created art as psychoanalysis" (1986, p. 1).[22] Schnitzler had intuitively grasped what Freud, the scientist, had only been able to discover with hard labor.

In Freud's work we encounter a tension between heredity and environment as factors explaining neuroses. He made a switch from environmental factors towards constitution coupled with fantasy when he abandoned the seduction theory and developed the libido theory. But he never made up his mind to privilege either side, and was unable to present a satisfactory solution for the dilemma.[23]

In Schnitzler's novels the same tension becomes apparent. In the *Traumnovelle*, Fridolin and Albertine lead a happily married life, until the husband spends a night away from home. His adventures, instigated by feelings of lust and aggression, are reflected by his wife in her dreams. Though not acted out in reality, her wishes are as equally promiscuous and aggressive as Fridolin's, and the couple starts thinking about their married life. Are they as happy and secure as they thought they were? Suddenly they are faced with a crossroads. One way leads to a monotonous marriage with, at best contentment but no real happiness. The real desires must remain unsatisfied; bourgeois life proves to be a facade, it offers security and respectability while real feelings have to be denied. The other road is more passionate, but giving passion free play is not without its dangers. Not only are lust and aggression difficult to reconcile with bourgeois conventions, but Fridolin and Albertine have good reason to fear for their marriage when they examine their intentions. They seem unable to control the chaos of feelings within themselves. The novel ends with their choosing marriage. Or should one say, instead of speaking of a choice, they are caught in the daily grind again?

Kenneth Segar (1973) has interpreted the *Traumnovelle* as consisting of two distinct poetic structures, "one expressing man's freedom to achieve a moral triumph over the powers of darkness, the other contradictorily showing the ultimately determined nature of character" (p. 123). We can view the characters from the perspective of freedom, where they experience a fairy tale of chaos and lust, but also from the perspective of psychological naturalism. "A chain of psychological determination is a different, but equally valid view of how the sober physician and paterfamilias comes to involve himself in a sexual orgy" (p. 125). And finally, is not the ethical decision to stay within the confines of marriage (as traditionally understood) determined by cravings for security and fear of chaos?

The duality appears in other novels with a different emphasis. In *Frau Bertha Garlan* we meet a widow who is content but not happy in her dull life until she gradually becomes engrossed by fantasies about a lover from her youth. Again, the story ends in disillusion: the ideals are not fulfilled in reality; Bertha ends up pondering the injustice done to women both by nature (she fears pregnancy) and morality. Bourgeois morality proves to be persistent, at least in Viennese social life which Schnitzler describes so well.[24]

Schnitzler analyzes the problems inherent in this duality in his aphorisms on psychoanalysis. When psychoanalysis views man as determined by universal laws of development, it is no longer able to understand individual developments. For these depend on a certain freedom from general mechanisms. "Precisely because of the fact that psychoanalysis generalizes its theories, e.g. the oedipus complex, it sacrifices their importance. If it really were the fate of every human being to love his mother and to hate his father, then this circumstance would be a phenomenon of human development like any other, like getting teeth, puberty, etc. -- and becomes uninteresting" (Schnitzler 1976, p. 278). If such phenomena occurred only in abnormal cases, they could explain certain individual features, not when they are universal. Also, the process of interpretation is tricky: "Using the mechanisms of reversal, displacement, and sublimation, [psychoanalysis] changes the limits of interpretation (*Deutungsgrenzen*) so much into the arbitrary, that any control becomes impossible, and any explanation could be replaced by its exact opposite. Also, the fact that psychoanalysis transgresses so soon into the unconscious is a sign of its weakness. It feels that the conscious could interfere, or sometimes even falsify its statements" (ibid). Psychoanalysis is caught in a dilemma. When it presupposes the determination of psychical processes - which is perfectly reasonable, even necessary, from a scientific point of view- it cannot explain such processes in individuals by recourse to general laws. One must inevitably study the personal history and the idiographic circumstances. Then it is not difficult to understand and to provide interpretations, even less so when one can resort to unconscious motives. But here the logic of explanation loses its grip. Freud is so immersed in the subjective individual uses of freedom, that he succumbs to his own subjectivity. There is no natural end to interpreting. We can conclude that Schnitzler shared Kraus' and Popper's concern with the use of psychoanalysis as an explanatory science, where it really only has to offer possibilities of interpretation. The latter are interesting enough: "Psychoanalysis is seductive for both doctor and patient".[25]

This section has reviewed three positions critical to Freud. Kraus spoke from an ethical point of view. Is it permissible to conflate scientific knowledge with ethical judgements? No, was the answer.

Psychoanalysis creates an ideology, it uses science as mere rhetoric: this is dangerous in public life. Popper pointed to the dangerous effects of an immunization against criticism within science. Being able to understand everything means that one explains nothing. The attitude of analysts, both within scientific discourse and towards their patients, is in danger of becoming uncritical and untestable. This is intolerable within the scientific realm. Schnitzler focused on an anthropological problem: how can we approach man if he is both determined and responsible? In literature, the two points of view seem to be reconcilable, but in psychoanalysis it is virtually impossible, as psychoanalysis deals with individual life.

These are basically negative contributions. Problems are pointed out, problems that seem to touch the foundations of psychoanalysis. It is interesting to note the parallels between these reflections and the criticisms raised by the scientific community as reviewed earlier in this article. Let us now turn to some more positive bearings on the problem.

4. *Hermeneutical conceptions found in the work of A.A. Grünbaum and Ludwig Wittgenstein*

The most sophisticated early expression of the hermeneutical nature of psychoanalysis, combined with a critique of its claims to universality, is found in the work of A.A. Grünbaum. Abraham Anton Grünbaum was born in Odessa in 1885. He was trained as a philosopher and an experimental psychologist in Leipzig where he worked with Wundt, and in Würzburg where he wrote his dissertation under Külpe. Between World War I and II, he held positions at the Dutch Universities of Utrecht and Amsterdam.[26] He died in 1932. Grünbaum was one of the few psychologists who were more than superficially acquainted with psychoanalysis. A paper on the psychoanalysis of dreaming, written in 1915, testifies both to his insight in and his critical attitude towards Freud's *Interpretation of Dreams*. He points out that the correspondence between dream work and dream interpretation contains a circularity, and makes clear that interpretations of dreams may be convincing, but always leave open the possibility of other interpretations. The method of free association provides a way of deciphering meanings, but also a way of attaching new meanings to dreams or other phenomena under consideration. One does not know where to stop the chain of associations and start the process of interpretation. These cautionary remarks on interpretative work are further amplified in a contribution by a reader dedicated to the impact of psychoanalysis on science and society, which appeared in 1928. Here Grünbaum claims that psychoanalysis is not a natural science, as Freud claims, but an entirely different kind of knowledge. Psychoanalysis must not try to be accepted by traditional forms of thinking: it must emphasize its revolutionary character in a thorough analysis of its own foundations. It is understandable that Freud looked upon the natural sciences as the ideal form of knowledge; but in his actual work he created a different kind of knowledge which might be called a technosophy instead of technology (scientia). Psychoanalysis is a tèchne in the sense that it is based upon practical experiences and involves practical capacities: the necessity of a learning analysis is peculiar to psychoanalytic theory. Apart from that, analytical thinking results in idiographic knowledge, valid in an individual case and difficult to generalize. And lastly, analytic knowledge transforms its object; it not only perfoms a mirror-function or delivers accurate descriptions, but it constitutes reality.[27]

This so-called 'ontological significance' of psychoanalytic thought forms a convincing argument for the adequacy of Grünbaum's epistemological evaluation. For how could a theory which, according to many, has only dubious value as a scientific construction, exert such an enormous influence on culture and society in our century?

The last question was also posed by Ludwig Wittgenstein (1889-1951). Like Schnitzler and Grünbaum, he had been struck by the seductiveness of psychoanalysis, and as with Kraus, the easy use analysts sometimes made of Freud's insights was repulsive to him.[28] The basic idea, ascribed by Wittgenstein to Breuer, is alright: "Freud's idea: In madness the lock is not destroyed, only altered; the old key can no longer unlock it, but it could be opened by a differently constructed key" (Wittgenstein 1977; diary remark from 1938). Problems arise when we ask for the nature of such a key and expect the wrong results in its use. "In a way having oneself psychoanalyzed is like eating from the tree of knowledge. The knowledge acquired sets us (new) ethical problems; but contributes nothing to their solution" (1939). "Freud has performed a disservice with his fantastical pseudo-explanations (precisely because they are brilliant). (Now any ass has these pictures available to use in 'explaining' symptoms of illness.)" (1946)[29]

Freud's explanations are brilliant, but they are not real explanations. Had they been real explanations, then "any ass" could have subsumed new phenomena under the laws discovered. But this is not the case. "What is intriguing about a dream is not its causal connection with events in my life, etc., but rather the impression it gives of being a fragment of a story -- a very vivid fragment to be sure -- the rest of which remains obscure"(1948). Freud claimed he offered something more than puzzle-solving strategies: his was an explanatory theory of dreaming, including techniques for the interpretation of dreams. He presented certain hypotheses as general laws or universal functions. Wittgenstein counters: "I think it might be regarded as a basic law of natural history that wherever something in nature 'has a function', 'serves a purpose', the same thing can also be found in circumstances where it serves no purpose and is even 'dysfunctional'. If dreams sometimes protect sleep, you can count on their sometimes disturbing it; if dream hallucination sometimes serves a plausible purpose (of imaginary wish fulfillment), count on it doing the opposite as well. There is no 'dynamic theory of dreams'". (Remark written in 1948).

Wittgenstein suggests that we can interpret dreams like stories. He has no objections against interpretations as such. Freud was brilliant in this art of interpretation. What Wittgenstein dismisses is Freud's claim that his interpretations are on one level with causal explanations and his tendency to hypothesize universal laws in the psychological domain. When his followers start using the 'techniques' and 'scientific hypotheses', they are misled about the nature of Freud's work. An interpretative discipline poses as a natural science.

5. *Conclusions*

The psychoanalytic research program was criticized in its first stage from different angles for its ambiguous character: it claimed to be an empirical-analytical science, but actually it was a hermeneutical enterprise. Due to the closed character of the psychoanalytic movement, the research program could not absorb arguments of this type, and until well after World War II the authority of Freud in all matters was almost never questioned. During the past decades, however, a more liberal attitude towards theoretical matters became possible within the movement, with the curious result that many analysts implicitly and probably unconsciously seemed to agree with arguments that were formulated by "The Opposition" 60 years ago.[30]

How are we to evaluate the onset of this 'liberalization'? I feel it is the only way to avoid petrification of psychoanalytic theory. It forms an impetus to new developments and makes it possible for psychoanalysis to absorb insights from other disciplines. Yet why did this development take place so late? Could it have occurred within Freud's lifetime, if he had wished so? Or would it have been too great a danger for the unity of the movement and the disciplinary matrix? I must leave the answers to these questions open here.

One could speculate, however, that there is a meaningful relation between the hermeneutic character of psychoanalysis, on the one hand, and the vast influences it has exerted on Western society and culture, on the other. Psychoanalysis demolished old dead metaphors and has opened up new viewpoints.[31] Using this terminology, it is only another step to view psychoanalysis as an example of what Gergen (1982) has called "generative theory". In Chapter 4 of this volume I will expound this notion more extensively. The question remains the same for different fields of psychological thought: what are the possibilities for research and theorizing from a non-empiricist perspective?

It is this question that Freud couldn't solve on the meta-level, though he no doubt answered it very creatively on the practical level. Something will be said about his work on dream interpretation in Chapter 7. In that field too the basic question remains the same. If psychoanalysis does not offer us regular empirical-analytical results, are we then confronted with an alternative type of knowledge that has come into its own? In the next chapter, basically the same epistemological question is asked and answered in different ways by the Dutch psychologist Johannes Linschoten. The question asked of such modern conceptions of psychological theorizing seems to be the same as the one which bothered Freud and his critics: "If it is not a science, what else can it be?"

3

THE CASE OF JOHANNES LINSCHOTEN'S APOSTASY: PHENOMENOLOGICAL VERSUS EMPIRICAL-ANALYTICAL PSYCHOLOGY

Contents:

Introduction

Twenty-five years after his death, Johannes Linschoten (1925-1964) has not yet been forgotten by Dutch psychology. Almost everyone is familiar with his work *Idolen van de Psycholoog* (*Idols of the Psychologist*) which appeared posthumously in 1964, the year of his death.[1] This study is a perceptive and still very readable defence of the empirical-analytical method in psychology against a number of different schools of thought which Linschoten considers unscholarly or unscientific, and against common everyday prejudice. It has played a role in creating the identity of Dutch psychology. A second work is less well-known: I am referring to *Op weg naar een fenomenologische psychologie* (*Towards a Phenomenological Psychology*) (1959), in which Linschoten discusses William James as a precursor of phenomenology. During the time of writing, Linschoten was part of a representative group of phenomenologists at the University of Utrecht. How do we explain the fact that Linschoten, as a prominent member of the "Utrecht School", was initially one of those who defended the notion of a phenomenological psychology, but subsequently and almost immediately afterwards revealed himself as an advocate of a methodology based on experiments and a fervent opponent of phenomenology? Even though we know that in psychology schools regularly replace each other, such a sudden personal switch remains tantalizingly mysterious. Should we look at Linschoten's personal life for an explanation?

These questions contain a relevance transcending an individual psychologist's biography. In what follows it will be claimed that both present-day phenomenological psychology and empirical-analytical psychology can profit from the arguments which Linschoten first embraced and later abandoned. In order to eludicate the questions posed above, we will have to trace Linschoten's development and to then place this in relation to Dutch psychology after the Second World War. What precisely did Linschoten's notion of phenomenology consist of, and how did his thinking about the fundamental principles of psychology develop in the course of his life?

I want to argue and demonstrate that Linschoten's development is characterized by a constant search for certainty in scientific knowledge. As I see it, it is in this craving for certainty that the continuity of his thinking rests. It led him to believe that the essence of phenomena can in principle be understood. Initially Linschoten thought that the phenomenological perspective was the single best indicator for apprehending and fathoming phenomena. After a period of transition during which he doubted the possibility of absolute knowledge and queried phenomenology, he decided that the empirical-analytical scientific method, which proceeds by means of rigorous reduction of the world into unrelated variables, was the most suitable one. Of course this implies a change in his epistemology and his conception of methodology. At the same time, however, it signifies a return to the ahistorical and realist Husserlian ontology to which he had adhered earlier.

2. *The Phenomenological Beginnings (1951-1956)*

In one of Linschoten's first publications, *Inleiding tot de Psychologie* (*Introduction to Psychology*) (1951) written together with B.J. Kouwer, he addresses a number of problems and opinions which remain representative throughout his later work. First of all there is the question regarding the problem of psychology as a science: How does psychological knowledge differ or distinguish itself from ordinary knowledge? Secondly, this early work affords insight into Linschoten's erudition and the range of his knowledge of psychology and its related disciplines. Thirdly and finally, this work, in its treatment of a number of schools of psychology, demonstrates very clearly Linschoten's affinity with "phenomenological psychology". The latter may be explained as a consequence of the prevailing attitude at Utrecht immediately after the war when Linschoten studied psychology there. Immediately after the war, Dutch psychology had not yet developed into an independent subject or discipline. In Germany one could speak of a clearly-defined professional identity before the Second World War. In the Netherlands psychology only gained independent status after empirical psychology became an academic subject by law in 1952. From 1942 on it had been possible to acquire a B.A. or M.A. in psychology, but the discipline was formally still part of the discipline of philosophy. It was not until 1964 that a faculty of social sciences was established in which subjects such as psychology, sociology, and pedagogy achieved autonomous status[2].

Linschoten was a student of F.J.J. Buytendijk (who was a nationally-known professor of general and theoretical psychology) and M.J. Langeveld (professor of pedagogy and developmental psychology). Both adhered to phenomenological ideas. Other influential Utrecht phenomenologists were the professor of law W.P.J. Pompe, and the professor of medicine H.C. Rümke. In 1949 Jhr. D.J. van Lennep was appointed full professor. He too applied phenomenological methods to several branches of psychology. Therefore, we can say that Linschoten's training was phenomenological in orientation.[3]

As I said earlier, the study of psychology had not yet been detached from philosophy. "There is no undivided psychology as an independent subject, there only are a number of people who call themselves 'psychologists', and who each for himself or herself consider *their* psychology to be 'the' psychology," Linschoten lets an outsider say (1951, p. 7). He admits this is a difficult point owing to the fact that psychology has not yet found its definitive shape. The subject originated, after all, from a wide range of disciplines. Its first consideration is common everyday life. "Psychology begins and ends with insight into *human nature*, with understanding our fellow-men" (*ibid.*, p. 8). A second source of non-scientific psychological insight is found in the works of poets and novelists. As third and fourth influence, Linschoten mentions religious consciousness and philosophical thought. In the fifth place, he mentions science as a source of psychological ideas and methods. Thus physiological methods were introduced into psychology. "Full of optimism one began 'measuring the soul'. This impulse lasted far into this century; especially in the United States it is still current" (*ibid.*, p. 12). Behaviorism was not yet popular in the Netherlands then, and certainly not in Utrecht. Finally Linschoten points to psychology's ties with psychopathology. He lists these sources of psychological thought to make clear how the inner division of psychology came about. His intention, however, is to rediscover a unity in the diversity by means of a search for the original psychological question. After a discussion of psychology of consciousness, behaviorism, and Gestalt psychology, Linschoten suggests a reorientation of psychology. "More and more the awareness increases that man is not a thing, not a machine which one can take apart into its component parts, but indeed an organic being that can only be understood in its totality" (1951, p. 88-89). It is not sufficient to know mankind physiologically, neither is it enough to separate consciousness into its elements or to understand human behavior in terms of a mechanical chain of reactions. The existing schools are deficient: "in order to understand man, one should consider him in relation to his context and situation, and try to fathom the structure of meaning of human situations. The principle of a scientific psychology rests not in the study of isolated experience or behavior, but in the context and situation" (*ibid.*).

It is remarkable that psychoanalysis is not mentioned in this survey of psychological schools, and that the interpretative humanities, such as Dilthey developed them, are hardly mentioned. This choice seems more self-evident when one considers Linschoten's reservations with regard to idiographic knowledge and the associated danger of relativism. At that moment he was looking for a solution to the problems he had outlined in phenomenological psychology.

3. *Phenomenological Psychology*

Psychology of consciousness and behaviorism had arrived at a dead end because they objectified consciousness or behavior as a thing or process. Linschoten looks to Husserl's phenomenology for a possibility of renewing one's thinking about psychology. A principal consideration is that in his everyday or natural attitude [*Einstellung*], man is not an isolated being but lives in his world. As a subject, man is not distinct from his environment but submerged in the situation in which he finds himself. Psychology might take it as its aim to investigate how man experiences the world. In doing so, the hidden preconception which characterizes objectifying schools of psychology is circumvented. Experience and behavior are no longer analyzed or considered to be things - quantifiable entities with causal connections. This latter kind of inquiry miscarried again and again because the true psychological questions remained untouched.

In a phenomenological psychology the question about experience is given new relevance. It is this query which offers itself as experience and world, about the organization of meaning. In this given situation the question does not consider objective matters concerning cause and effect. The question is how the situation is experienced. The reevaluation of experience is accompanied by a renewed interest in physical experience. My body, under normal circumstances, is not a thing, but my grasp on the world is. The description of a concrete situation consistently refers back to the person for whom that situation exists. Thus experience and behavior may be integrated. "And thus it is possible for a phenomenological psychology to be a psychology of behavior and consciousness at the same time, because it takes its beginning in considering the situation, and not in 'objectively perceptible behavior' or the 'introspectively perceptible phenomena of consciousness'" (1951, p. 99). The postulated unity of perception and movement is defended by Linschoten with an appeal to Von Weizsäcker and Merleau-Ponty.

Linschoten concludes his contributions to the book with the concession that the phenomenological school of psychology is still young; but once one has acquired the insight that man is not a *thing*, the way is open for a new psychology, which takes as its point of departure the meaning of man's situation and his life world. "The development of psychology still lies largely ahead", Linschoten writes with the optimism which characterizes psychologists of that era. He keeps that confident belief in the future of psychology until the end of his life.

During this same period he publishes his first articles. For the larger part these are phenomenological analyses along the lines of the program outlined above. "Logische en phenomenologische analyse der bewegingsverschijnselen" (Logical and Phenomenological Analysis of Phenomena of Movement) (1950), "Over de Humor" (On Humour) (1951), and "Over het inslapen" (On Falling Asleep) (1952) show us how a phenomenologist works in practice. The young assistant professor has an easy style of writing and an impressive erudition. Concrete descriptions of, for instance, situations of falling asleep and sleeplessness are derived from literary and philosophical texts from the hands of Proust, Baudelaire, Poe, Nietzsche, Sartre, Rilke, and Bachelard. However, the present-day reader might very well fall asleep while following Linschoten's analysis of these examples because they tend to be tedious. There seems to be a discrepancy between the author's intentions and what he actually accomplishes.

Linschoten's study of falling asleep provides an example. He begins with stating that falling asleep is not treated as a problem in psychological handbooks. "If we want to know why we are tortured thus, and how sleeplessness should be combatted, then nothing remains us but a *conversation with falling asleep*. We want to query the phenomenon and understand it in its essential structure" (1952, p. 208). A short summary of the problems which such a conversation entails follows - thus the loss of consciousness before sleep is impenetrable to theoretical reflection. As a consequence, "sleep" is understood as a deep dreamless state, and the dreaming consciousness is excluded from analysis for the time being. "Notwithstanding this [Linschoten argues] an analysis of falling asleep is not meaningless, as I hope to demonstrate in the following pages" (p. 209). Then follow 50 pages of phenomenological analysis of falling asleep in general, illustrated by literary examples. The methodological reflection which Linschoten adds is interesting because of the distinction he makes between psychological research and phenomenological reflection.

"*I* am asleep and *I* am awake; and in the change from one to the other my history unfolds itself as *mine*. This personal meaning and determination of the situation in which I fall asleep we should not lose sight of in the analysis of falling asleep in a general sense as a relationship between the person and the world. To the psychologist this analysis [the *philosophical* analysis of falling asleep in general] remains a preliminary state that has to be transcended before he arrives at his proper task, which is characterized or defined by the return to the concrete person. The psychological nature of the question which guided this inquiry implied that we had to limit ourselves to the individual person. In the light of a pure phenomenological analysis the preceding [the analysis of concrete examples] remains locked into psychological naivety which ought to be transcended before the real analysis of the act with regard to I-myself-in-my-origin can begin. Only then will it be possible to ground our analysis in a general theory of intentionality. Thus this contribution to phenomenological psychology remains a preliminary investigation in the light of a pure phenomenology" (1952, p. 259).

This quotation becomes clear when we see the distinction between a pure phenomenological intuition of essence and phenomenological psychology. It is not the personal history or the concrete example which provide the object of study for phenomenological analysis. Phenomenology has higher aims: it wants to penetrate *falling asleep in general*. When it focusses on concrete examples, this is only a preliminary stage, even one testifying to naivety. Expectations are high, and consequently the results of the inquiry can only be labelled preliminary conclusions. It is not surprising, then, that Linschoten's sequence of examples threatens to bore one from time to time. In themselves they are not of real interest to Linschoten the phenomenologist: they only provide raw material for a later intuition of essence. We note a discrepancy between the pretensions of a phenomenological intuition of essences and the concrete results of a phenomenological psychology. Let us investigate another example.

4. *The Function of Examples*

In the course of his argument Linschoten provides many examples derived from literary sources. Individual events or occurrences are not given thorough analysis or interpretation, however. They are only interesting as illustrations of general insights or essential characteristics. "Falling asleep thus means to disengage oneself from what approaches, to leave things to take their course, and to distantiate oneself without concern .... Alexander the Great slept so soundly the evening of the battle against Darius, that he had to be called three times because the hour of battle was approaching .... Montaigne was so intrigued by these facts .... that he devoted one of his essays to sleep. Indeed, this is the irritating secret of falling asleep: one is indifferent to everything - or, what amounts to the same, the world recedes and loses its claim" (1952, p. 240).

There is a strong suggestion that Linschoten, due to his phenomenological insight into the essence of sleep, is no longer capable of wondering about such situations. Alexander's falling asleep only illustrates a general phenomenon. Could it not be possible, however, that the readability of Montaigne's essays (compared to, for instance, those of Linschoten), is because the French philosopher was capable of continued wonder about concrete occasions and events? Is it perhaps true that his examples continue to interest us after 400 years because he manages to make their relationship clear without resorting to generalization? At any rate, the question is what to do with the general structures of essence presented by Linschoten.

The example of Alexander the Great does not imply that the general is able to distantiate himself without care from the events of the following day. We are interested in the specific circumstances that cause someone to lie awake at such a crucial moment. Historians try to find out such matters because they often prove to be related to important historical circumstances.[4] But this question is not the one which preoccupies Linschoten. He sticks to the general aspect which to him is the essential one.

The question is whether a phenomenological analysis is useful for the psychologist who sees himself confronted with concrete examples of sleeplessness. Linschoten's reply to the question how we should fall asleep: "ensure a sense of comfort and security, and don't do anything" is, in its generality, at once completely true and completely useless. Perhaps he himself also senses this, since he continues: "But not in the *terms* of this analysis lies the essence of falling asleep. This analysis has only achieved its aim if it is continually confronted with the phenomena, and confirmed in unmediated perception (1952, p. 260). The problem is that characteristics of essence may manifest themselves in countless ways: "My personal relationship to the other and to the community determines the way in which the situation of my falling asleep constitutes itself as one of security. But it is the essential quality of security, which manifests itself a million times, that allows me to fall asleep" (p. 244).

Here it is as if deep in his heart Linschoten doubts Husserl's notion of intuition of essence, and is recommending a concrete investigation of phenomena in their variety. That would allow a concrete examination of essential insights which would probably end in a total rejection of the very notion that the essence of things lies in unchanging common characteristics. Linschoten did indeed arrive at that conclusion, as we shall see below.[5] His study of the process of falling asleep concludes with a reference to the myth of a primal stillness: "And the lulling melody that had been softer than the wind-harp of Aeolus, ... it died little by little away, in murmurs growing lower and lower, until the stream returned, at length, utterly, into the solemnity of its original silence" (E.A. Poe, cited in Linschoten 1952, p. 261).

5. *Experimental Psychology*

The year 1952 also witnessed the publication of Linschoten's study "Experimentelle Untersuchung der sog. induzierten Bewegung" ("Experimental Research into So-called Induced Movement") in the journal *Psychologische Forschung*. The experiments were carried out in 1948-49, and the article was completed in 1950. As Schenk (1982) indicates, it was not unusual in Utrecht to conduct experiments from a phenomenological perspective. Linschoten considers it a challenge to interpret the results of his activities phenomenologically.

In a dark room, subjects are presented with two figures of which one is moving, without being given a framework to interpret this movement. Thus it becomes impossible to determine objectively what is moving, and the judgment of phenomena proves to be independent of the relations between the figures. Perceived movement is seen in relation to the meaningful interpretation which the individual assigns to the figures, that is, puts into the situation. A concrete explanation of the phenomenon of induced movement, in other words, demands a phenomenological analysis of the individual relationship of the observer to the figures. Linschoten continues his experiments on perception in his dissertation (1956a).[6] He also writes the chapters on general experimental psychology in Kohnstamm's *Inleiding in de Psychologie* (*Introduction to Psychology*).

Linschoten edits the *liber amicorum* for Buytendijk's 65th birthday. *Persoon en Wereld* (*Person and World*) (1953)[7] is a highlight for Dutch (that is, largely Utrecht) psychology. Langeveld, Van Lennep, Rümke, Kouwer, J.J. Dijkhuis, Van den Berg, Vermeer, and others contribute. Linschoten's contribution is called "Aspecten van de sexuele incarnatie" ("Aspects of the Sexual Incarnation"), and questions the body as vehicle and medium of existence. Inspired by the ideas of the French phenomenologist Merleau-Ponty, he accuses Husserl that in his rediscovery and explanation of the *Cogito* he has considered the body merely as an object of intentional acts. To a philosophical anthropology this premise is no more fruitful than the conception of the body as *res extensa*. After all, what matters is the body as it lives and experiences. Indeed, there is much which transcends the strictly individual level. After all, the male or female body, each in its own way, facilitates certain kinds of experience while precluding others. Thus Linschoten has chosen a more "timeless" subject for his phenomenological analysis than, for instance, Van Lennep who discusses the hotel room and the psychology of driving a car; Rümke who discusses the discontent with one's own nose; or Langeveld who writes about the secret places in the life of the child. On the other hand, it is obvious that sexual relationships and how they are experienced, differ from culture to culture and time to time. Linschoten is conscious of the fact that sexual relationships may take different forms than the one he describes, because *in concreto* an "endless variety of formal expression" is possible. But this variety is possible within the parameters which the body, "this provisional sketch of existence", opens up (1953a, p. 125). A brief example may help to elucidate the nature of this space and its margins: Linschoten discusses a theory which regards the penis as the most distinctive instrument of the male body. He disagrees with this view because the penis is precisely the opposite of an instrumental organ. One cannot use it to "perform" things with. It is not a manipulative organ, but at best merely a manipulable one. Biologically man is defined by a penis; psychologically he is not. "Psychologically we understand man as man primarily in terms of his masculine existence, *which is also a possible existence for the biological woman*: an existence defined by work ...." (pp. 102-103, italics added). We note here that Linschoten is conscious of the fact that biology in itself does not determine anything, and that, moreover, it is the concrete embodiment of social tasks (performed by either men or women) which is subject to change and historical circumstance, which lends notions such as "masculine" and "feminine" their specific connotation. In the "Conclusion" to the *Liber Amicorum*, Linschoten argues again, in a philosophical reflection, that each interpretation or explanation begins with the specific and variable and proceeds to the fundamental and permanent. Physical science reaches its goal by means of a reduction of the given to underlying processes; phenomenology by means of making certain general intentional structures explicit. "Faithful to its principle [phenomenology] does not look in the specific and variable for what lies behind or underneath it, but for the intentional structure which it already contains" (1953b, p. 252). This is not a causal explanation; "the phenomenological explanation is *a making explicit*, it moves in a hermeneutical circle".

It is regrettable that Linschoten disregards the implications of his words. We note that he regards the "dialectic of person and landscape" as the central problem of psychology. He refrains, however, from also applying the hermeneutical circle to the relationship existing between the person conducting the experiment and the subjects of the test. Doing this might bring scholarly explanation in conflict with current notions of objectivity, but it might also enhance its fidelity to the nature of the object. Of course, "a phenomenological psychology is critical of a scientific psychology". The original question, however, remains the same throughout: "all psychology enquires about man as he functions in his existence on earth, as he is continuously *becoming* in his history as a person" (p. 253).

From this it may appear that man needs to be understood as a historical being. Is psychology a historical discipline which gathers historically-determined (and hence relative) knowledge? This is not the conclusion drawn by Linschoten. Incidentally, this historical view of knowledge has not gained currency in later, post-War developments in phenomenological psychology (Giorgi, 1982). Usually it is identified with Heidegger's criticism of Husserl (cf. De Boer 1978) and the hermeneutical approach to the humanities (cf. see chapters 5 and 6 in this volume), which could mean the abandonment of, rather than variations within phenomenology.[8] Anyway, Linschoten appears to treasure the notion that a phenomenological psychology, fully in accord with Husserl's ideas, must eventually arrive at objective knowledge of relations of essence. This provides a different type of knowledge than that acquired by means of a positivist reduction of the human being. It is indeed *possible* to reduce man, but there is more to man than that. Linschoten is drawn by the transcendental, and he hopes to be able to investigate this almost indefinable realm which has hitherto been the object of poets, novelists, and philosophers, from a scientific point of view. Phenomenology remains a task with provisional modest results. In his inaugural address as professor of experimental general psychology at the University of Utrecht on December 2, 1957, he sketches the outlook of a phenomenological psychology in contradistinction to the dominant -- though not current everywhere in the Netherlands -- empirical-analytical psychology.

6. *Prediction and Understanding: 1957-1964*

Edgar Allen Poe invented the figure of the detective Monsieur C. Auguste Dupin, a man of extraordinary powers. "Imagine the surprise of his friend when M. Dupin, after having walked side by side in silence for fifteen minutes, suddenly, and without apparent cause says to him: "He is a very little fellow, that's true, and would do better for the Théâtre des Variétés". In these words Dupin articulates the thought which his friend had been trying to formulate about a certain actor in himself and merely for himself" ("A Gentle Force", Inaugural Address Utrecht, 1957e, p. 3).[9]

Poe presents us here with the ideal of the psychologist as associational psychology has articulated it. Psychology attains its perfection as a science if it is capable of predicting, with the aid of laws of association, how a person will think, feel, and act throughout life. With regret, Linschoten concludes that Dupin seems naturally capable of things which the techniques of psychology have still not made possible. This concern with the practical applicability of the discipline is new to Linschoten, and probably should be seen as related to his appointment to the professorship. He became head of a lab and a training institute, and perhaps this made him more conscious than he used to be of a certain responsibility for the manner in which psychology legitimizes itself.

Linschoten points out in his inaugural address that associational psychology is still the dominant school in contemporary psychology. This is the heritage of Hume who thought the elements of the psychical connected by means of a "gentle force" on the example of the Newtonian force of gravity in physics. But is our "human nature" truly a Humean nature? "Should this be the case -- so be it", Linschoten answers. "It is not the task of the psychologist to attack or defend world views or conceptions about human nature in the realm of political debate. But it is his task to ensure that his theories, which are irrevocably appropriated by the community, are adequate to that which they pretend to describe and explain" (p. 16).

The second part of the address makes a plea for an increased adequacy of psychological theories. This will become possible if psychological theorizing takes the structure of historically developed forms of human existence into account. Psychology is predicated upon it and will have to deal with that structure adequately. Human reality, unlike Humean reality, consists of relations of meaning between the contents of experience. These phenomena cannot be simplified in such a way that what remains may clearly be reduced to bodily processes. One must make an appeal to the analysis of language and meaning. Psychology must find its way back to "the situational reality of every practice and experience" (p. 23). This reality is full of internal relations, which we may compare to pebbles situated in a forest to mark a path. The psychologist is someone who only wants to investigate the proximity in space and time of the pebbles, and forgets that the path was traced by someone. With this image Linschoten concludes his plea for a different psychology which does not only acknowledge relationships of meaning, but also acknowledges their historical character. But the "Ladies and Gentlemen Students of Psychology" are admonished that the experimental aspect should not be lost. "A psychological experiment without phenomenological analysis is a step in the dark. A phenomenological psychology without experiment is, even though probably not worse, probably not much better than the empirical associational psychology" (p. 27).

Looking at Linschoten's publications between 1955 and 1960, we note about fifteen short articles on concrete problems and professional practice. To list a few examples: The psychology of sports; The psychologist and professional secrecy; Thoughts about "instinct" and birth control; What is living?; and Parapsychology and ordinary psychology. The more concrete the problem, the more practical his considerations, and the more readable the articles become. After thirty years, it is precisely the phenomenological analyses of essences which make the most dated impression. The critical review of *Metabletica* (*The Changing Image of Man*) (1957) demonstrates that Linschoten takes a radically different view than its author J.H. van den Berg, and disapproves of his anti-scholarly approach. The book about problem children, *Psychische moeilijkheden* (*Psychological Problems*) (1956b), shows Linschoten as a practical psychologist with great empathy for children. Here we also note how he is aware of the precarious relationship between everyday knowledge and scholarly findings, as a quotation illustrates: "Psychological and psychiatric knowledge are spreading with increasing speed. To the extent that it improves the relationships between people, between adults, and between parents and children, this should be applauded. But this advantage is often attended by a disadvantage: the lack of certainty which arises when people acquire the feeling that others have more insight into their children than they themselves -- that the education of children is, in fact, a specialisation, and should be learned during a directed course of training . . . ." (p. 7) I will return to this notion later.

In 1959 the previously-mentioned study of the ideas of William James, *Op weg naar een fenomenologische psychologie* (*Towards a Phenomenological Psychology*) was published. Due to a lack of space, I cannot enter into a lengthy discussion of the phenomenological interpretation of James' psychology. I must restrict myself here to quoting a few of Linschoten's comments regarding James, which might equally apply to himself. The first is that James often experienced his own broadmindedness and lack of prejudice as inner division. "The whole does not add up to anything" (1959c, p. 25). A second comment concerns James' lack of satisfaction with his work: he writes to his publisher that his *Principles* proves two things: "'Ist that there is no such thing as a science of psychology, and 2nd, that W.J. is an incapable'" (p. 23). Linschoten praises James' courage of self-expression, even though he disagrees with his second point. The third reference of Linschoten's regarding James which I want to quote suggests that "James unites, like phenomenology, an extreme subjectivism with an extreme objectivism ... Thus we note James' unquestioning acceptance of the validity of the knowledge of physical science besides, and in addition to, a descriptive knowledge. Yes, he does not hesitate to affirm freedom and determinism of behavior and experience in one breath" (p. 189-190). Indeed, in a similar way

Linschoten himself also tries to unite the phenomenology of experience with the objectification of reality. However, the ambivalence which is implicit in this intention weighs heavily.

We have seen that up to this moment Linschoten has consistently argued that understanding of a meaningful life-world should be the point of departure of all psychological knowledge and insight. Research which does not depart from this premise is blind and aimless. Phenomenological analysis can help in the explanation of the life-world. Empirical-analytical reductions of reality, as they are necessary for experimental research, may provide relevant and useful information if one knows *what* one is reducing and *why*. Knowledge obtained by this method remains dependent upon the primary knowledge of the life-world, and hence it may be integrated with that knowledge without prohibiting problems. Linschoten uses the term "complementarity". However, what happens when one considers the power to predict as the only goal of psychology? Linschoten indicates that this scientific ideal has been an important motive in psychological theorizing, at least since the times of John Locke. To common and everyday thought, knowledge appears impressive and convincing when it enables one to predict future occurrences or situations. This equation of knowledge with insight into universal laws, and an attending power to predict and control, has become dominant in our culture. The power to understand meanings and the creativity to interpret concrete situations are less highly regarded and are also seen as extra-scientific. A psychology which intends to prove itself as a scholarly discipline will have to make an impression upon society. The connection with everyday thought about man, however paradoxical this may sound, could prove to be a disadvantage. The introduction of professional jargon, esoteric techniques, and abstract models of "man" may create an impressive distance and as such it may provide an advantage. In the long run, the degree to which all this provides us with skills to predict and control may be decisive for the success of psychology as a scientific discipline. Whether our insight into the relations of meaning in the life-world is enhanced is another question. With regard to that subject, Linschoten's phenomenological position leads to the inevitable tenet that stereotyping the power to predict as the only aim of a scientific psychology constitutes at least a reduction of the object, as well as the typical knowledge of psychology.

Towards a Phenomenological Psychology can be read as a process of growing conscious. Already William James sensed that two very different, hardly reconcilable approaches to psychology are possible. Different questions and diverging interests are at issue. Meanings cannot be deciphered by means of predictions; on the other hand, a sense of the relevance of the concrete does not provide techniques of control. Linschoten faces this dilemma and seems to grow more and more convinced that phenomenology will always remain on the way towards an elusive goal. He has investigated and studied countless concrete psychological questions and his answers were based on common sense. This remains unsatisfactory. Is it impossible for psychology to radically distinguish itself from common sense? Is there no way towards a "new psychology"?

7. *The Triumph of the Empirical-Analytical Method*

Goethe once said that "Man ist gegen nichts strenger als gegen erst abgelegte Irrtümer". This idea provides a perspective on Linschoten's last period. In the years 1960-1961 he published little. In 1963 a last defence of the inevitability of reflection upon the life-world appears entitled "Die Unumgänglichkeit der Phänomenologie" (The Indispensable Character of Phenomenology).[9] This article can be summarized as follows: reductive theories of reality are possible and have a necessary function in psychology, but they should not be seen as the only possible approach to reality. The behaviorist defending his notion of man as an organism, while disputing the postulate of "consciousness", nevertheless appeals to everyday matters of fact. "Consciousness is a fiction"? This statement presupposes a preceding concept of what consciousness is. The defence of scientific theories requires recourse to everyday speech. Science is a superstructure on the soil of the life-world, and in the description and analysis of this primary experience we cannot avoid phenomenology. A scientific approach to the world such as the behaviorist one opposes itself to the naivety of a psychology which describes experience and behaviors in common everyday speech which is soaked in mythology. But in defending its approach, it nevertheless must avail itself of this language soaked in mythology. [10] This does not mean, however, that psychology should keep pledging allegiance to the phenomenological notion of man. In this respect Linschoten has changed his view radically. [11]

"In contradistinction to some years ago, I am of the opinion that psychology, as all sciences, can only reach its aim by means of formalisation and quantification, by means of the experimental analysis of conditions and by means of the construction of models. In doing so its formalised professional vocabulary will have to diverge widely from ordinary speech. I regard phenomenology, in any case, as an indispensable preconception in this endeavour". (1963b, 182-183).

With this statement Linschoten's notion of phenomenology seems to have undergone a further change. Again he reflects upon a concrete analysis of forms of life which might replace the search for eternal verities. "Did not Husserl say that fiction is the source which feeds the knowledge of 'eternal verities'?" (p. 178). And again: "I consider the characterization of the life-world as a passive given as too dogmatic. Why would thinking in terms of hypotheses not also have a function in phenomenology? Why could its 'eternal verities' not be taken as *provisionally* eternal? It would make phenomenology's task to be an archeology of the life-world more easy" (p. 184). Linschoten also compares science to analytical games which operate in the frame of the world of experience (p. 179), while referring to Wittgenstein's *Blue and Brown Books*.

With this a relativization of both phenomenology and the sciences has been reached which might provide a stepping stone to a transition to a Wittgensteinian relativism of language games. However, in his final publications Linschoten shifts the ideal of absolute knowledge to the field of empirical-analytical psychology. This would never provide eternal verities, it is true, but it might be able, by means of unceasing critical reflection upon facts, to leave the mythologies of the *sensus communis* far behind. Thus it might be capable of enhancing the prestige of psychology.

In the year 1963, the article "Fenomenologie en psychologie" ("Phenomenology and Psychology") appeared, presenting a final reckoning with Husserlian phenomenology, which can only lead to a radically humanist approach. Linschoten states without much ado: It is "precisely in the positivist design that psychology is successful these days -- a success which considerably reduces its feelings of inferiority towards the exact sciences" (p. 113). Reductive models along positivist lines are fruitful. Why should we still pay attention to phenomenology? The ideas expressed in this article are worked out in more detail in *Idolen van de psycholoog* (*Idols of the Psychologist*) which appeared a year later, immediately after Linschoten's decease. This book consists of a collection of lectures which center around the continued confrontation between phenomenology and experimental psychology.

Here I shall focus on three problematic points. In the first place, Linschoten's defence of the fruitfulness of reductive models bears criticism. He readily admits that experimental psychology investigates an impoverished world. But to begin with this is inevitable -- it is impossible to investigate the relations between ten variables all at once -- and secondly it at least provides hard facts. Vigorously proceeding along these lines, many insignificant facts will together result in a theory on man. Now, twenty years later, we may well call this hope unfounded. The subsequent development of experimental psychology has made us aware of the problems of inductivism and of the mutability of man and cultures.[13]

Secondly: It is striking that Linschoten wishes to detach empirical-analytic psychology (he speaks of functionalizing and formalizing science) from the *sensus communis* or the everyday life-world. By doing this, he defends the thesis that quantification and reduction of phenomena do not contain a distortion of reality against the phenomenological perspective. "Psychology as a science can only come into its own when it frees itself of the anthropology of a *sensus communis* ..... The opinions which make up the *sensus communis* are the idols of the psychologist" (1964, pp. 56-60). This is a form of scientism which Linschoten shortly before, or even simultaneously, fought with strong arguments. At least it entails a predilection for one model of science over another. This choice is not given an articulate defence. The lack of argument could mean that he either naively believes in the empirical-analytical ontology which represents the world as analyzable and governed by laws, or that he is trying to avoid a philosophical defence of this methodology. On the other hand, however, his attacks upon the high-flown pretensions of phenomenological psychology are not unreasonable; but they fail to exclude the possibility of a more modest phenomenological psychology.

A third comment on *Idols* concerns the value of interpretative knowledge. For the later Linschoten, "knowledge" equals lawlike generalizations and deductive-nomological explanations. Once he also believed in the intuition of essences of phenomenology. Earlier we already concluded that idiographic knowledge, the judgment of a concrete situation or an individual human being, has never occupied an important place in Linschoten's concept of science. He always departed from the assumption that general knowledge can be applied to individual cases without problems. This can be illustrated using an example from psychoanalysis.

Freud continually presents interpretations of individuals and situations, of the meaning of symptoms, slips of the tongue, and of dreams. The *Interpretation of Dreams* (1900) consists of rules for and examples of the interpretation of dreams, with a more or less separate theory which is designed to explain dream processes. With regard to Freud too, we note that the knowledge which informs practice is not considered by himself as truly scientific.[14] The interpretations and the heuristics of interpretation must be based on a truly scientific theory couched in neurophysiological terms. It is striking that Linschoten never paid any attention to the hermeneutic aspects of psychoanalysis. In his phenomenological analysis "On Humour" (1951a), he points out that we may look for the psychological meaning of humour - regarding this, for instance, as a "mechanism of defence" or a "source of pleasure". This is a reductive reading of humour, as devised by Freud, to which he does not wish to subscribe. In a footnote he charmingly confesses "We absolutely fail to see how we could avail ourselves of this constructive theory in our research. Cf. S. Freud, *Jokes and their Relationship to the Unconscious* ...." (Linschoten 1951a, p. 606). The difference between Linschoten and Freud is, therefore, that the latter's work relates and analyzes a whole range of jokes, while the former writes a fairly unhumourous article full of abstract generalizations. The point of comparison is that both are preoccupied with the scientific character of their work. From that point of view, Linschoten eagerly surrendered the privilege of telling stories and describing psychological reality to the writers of fiction. He did demonstrate his erudition by citing many instances from novels, but he felt that the psychologist should stick to his trade. Freud, on the other hand, aimed at elucidating literature as well as his therapeutic interpretations by means of psychoanalytic theory. Linschoten avoided such an integrative approach.

Idols presents strong criticism of Freud's arbitrary manner of interpretation. An example from the *Psychopathology of Everyday Life*, forgetting the name Signorelli is given lengthy attention (1964, pp. 328-337). Freud analyzes his temporary forgetfulness by means of free association and the subsequent attribution of a motive. His reconstruction after the fact is that he had shortly before wanted to tell a story to a fellow traveller, but had on second thought decided not to do so, because he did not want to steer the conversation towards the topics of death and sexuality. Due to certain associational connections, the name "Signorelli" was also repressed.

Linschoten provides interesting commentary on this passage. Thus he argues that a reconstruction of the process after the fact need not be identical to its original course. In his eagerness to demonstrate the arbitrariness of all interpretation, he proceeds to free-associate himself to the names of Signorelli, Botticelli, and Boltraffio. With obvious relish he manages to produce three totally different reconstructions of the event. In his conclusion, he adheres closely to the view which has been ventured by many readers: Freud's interpretation is unconvincing. It seems to say more about the interpreter's desires and opinions than about the object of interpretation. Linschoten's line of argument, however, totally ignores the fact that Freud was interpreting a concrete situation which had happened to himself at some moment, and with regard to which certain associations occurred to *himself*. The interpretation and reconstruction provided are only valid for this individual case. Disregarding this, Linschoten summarizes Freud's reading as a general law: *always*, whenever someone cannot remember the name "Signorelli", the same explanation must be valid. That this is not the case is self-evident. Each concrete case must be interpreted within its own specific context.[15]

From this example it becomes clear that Linschoten can hardly envision an interpretative psychology oriented towards idiographic knowledge. When he speaks of science he is thinking of physical science oriented towards the discovery of general laws. The nature of the cultural sciences is never a point of discussion. Interpretation is subjective. This is a philosophical presupposition which in the course of Linschoten's metamorphosis from a phenomenologist into an empirical-analytical psychologist remains unchanged, though it is given thought. In this respect Linschoten is firmly rooted in the tradition of empirical psychology, which has tried to gain a reputation as a physical science of man since 1880. Phenomenology refrains from a radical break with this notion of self-identity, but it does point to the dependence of scientific language upon everyday language, with reference to Husserl's *Krisis der europäischen Wissenschaften*. Empirical-analytical science does not occupy itself with man's first nature then, as some of its adherents think, but with the formulation of theoretical concepts of the second order, which remain independent from the first-order concepts of everyday language.[16] This is a philosophical footnote to the status of research into the humanities and cultural sciences which must not be considered an argument against the empirical-analytical approach. The original way in which Linschoten conducts both his phenomenological analyses as well as empirical-analytical research testifies to this -- at least up to a certain moment. It would seem that in the lectures given during the last years of his life, published in *Idols of the Psychologist*, he was defending a purely experimental psychology. Not only would this seem inconsistent with his earlier viewpoint, it also seems contradictory to his simultaneous defence of phenomenology in the essay "The Indispensable Character of Phenomenology" (Linschoten 1963b). In conclusion, I will try to resolve this seeming contradiction and offer some speculative comments on Linschoten's change of course.

8. *Background to Linschoten's Change of Mind*

After the second World War, Dutch psychology became firmly established in the universities. The number of students mutiplied by ten. The number of professors increased less steeply, from eight before the war to 20 in the year 1960. As a consequence, the number of practising psychologists multiplied rapidly. In 1946 the Dutch Institute for Practising Psychologists had 36 members, in 1960 it listed almost 300. Psychologists acquired a position on the job market by outwitting the competition by means of a scholarly approach and technique.

Here the competition with graphology can serve as an example. This chapter from the post-War history of Dutch psychology has recently been described for the first time by Trudy Dehue.[18] In 1947 A.D. de Groot published an article in which he claimed that it was morally and scientifically irresponsible to evaluate people merely by means of a graphological analysis of personality. This critical attitude, shared by psychologists in general, generated a discussion during the fifties which increasingly drove graphology into a tight corner. The demand that its results should be verifiable seemed a reasonable one. Evaluation reports should enable predictions about future behavior or performance. The less graphology proved capable of offering the kind of knowledge enabling prediction, the more it ensconced itself in wholistic tenets, clinging to man's complexity supposedly inaccessible to scientific investigation. Psychology gained both on the level of theory as well as practice: theoretically because its demand of verifiability seemed essential according to contemporary epistemology and hence completely convincing; in practice because it seemed, in fact, better able to generate predictive knowledge than competing professions. The rise of empirical-analytic methods in psychology is therefore closely linked to the establishment of psychology at the universities in the period after World War II.

Is it surprising that given this situation Linschoten too would change his mind? Once appointed professor and free to determine his own course, he needed some time to liberate himself from the influence of his mentor Buytendijk - or so one might argue - but eventually he could not lag behind national and international developments. Phenomenology only lived on in the work and teachings of some older scholars, to die out completely. As a phenomenologist, Linschoten could only have played an atavistic role in the course of the rest of his career.

This argument may require some qualifying comments. First of all, Linschoten's change of mind seems especially radical. The term "conversion" has been used in this connection. Van Strien speaks of Linschoten's "apostasis" (1986, p. 106). This demands an explanation. Linschoten had always emphasized that phenomenology did not rule out experimental-quantifying research. He defended a qualified point of view, taking care not to lend phenomenology absolute status as the only possible empirical method. A similar point of view was taken by Strasser, who defended his phenomenological reflection as a psychological metatheory.[19]

Why then did Linschoten suddenly turn so violently upon his former fellow phenomenologists? The reason is that these were not open to the defence of a combination of empirical-analytic psychology and phenomenology. On the whole, they ignored or rejected the new empirical methods without qualification. Moreover, they remained locked in a form of philosophical thought which Linschoten considered inappropriate to psychology as an empirical science. One might think in this connection of Thomas Kuhn's observation that the transition from an immature preparadigmatic science to a mature paradigmatic one is always attended by the ending of philosophical discussions about the principles of the profession.[20]

"But there are always some men who cling to one or another of the older views, and they are simply read out of the profession, which thereafter ignores their work" (Kuhn 1962, p. 19). Thus Linschoten apparently thought that the discussion about philosophical problems in psychology had exhausted itself -- thus it ought to be carried on by philosophers. It is important, therefore, to draw a distinction between the practice of psychological research and philosophical reflection upon it. The methodology which Linschoten offered to his students in his lectures implied the defence of the independence and indispensability of empirical research. Philosophical reflection was not something to be engaged in by every student; its proper place was in the professional journals.

Linschoten himself describes his change of mind accurately in his article "The Indispensable Character of Phenomenology". He has lost all confidence in phenomenology as a scientific method. Like other (physical) sciences, psychology should formalize, quantify, experiment, and construct models. In other words, science becomes physical science, and psychology should not orient itself towards history, literature, or philosophy.

At the level of philosophical reflection, however, Linschoten remains prepared to acknowledge the value of phenomenology as a method of analysis and reflection. It can demonstrat the limited reach of objectifying psychologies, but also generate hypotheses about the life-world within which scientific theories are developed. The so-called "given" must be revealed as a myth. In this respect Linschoten may be considered a precursor of social constructionism.[21]

It is interesting,in his lectures to his students, to see Linschoten end his career as a rigorous advocate of scientific method, while not denying his philosophical awareness at the same time. It seems an experiment in thought: How far can one go with the consistent defence of a train of thought? Precisely because he knew the arguments against scientism so well -- in his inaugural address he had masterfully defeated it in the guise of associational psychology -- he was able to defend the empirical-analytical approach intelligently and creatively. Had Linschoten's health been better and had he not died prematurely, his final work would without doubt have been a transitional one on the way to a next intellectual position. Whether he would have wanted to embrace a phenomenological psychology ever again is doubtful. Less doubtful is that he would have grown sensitive to the limitations of the empirical-analytic approach in the course of time. In this respect *Idols* radiates a certain optimism which is characteristic of the pioneering times of hard methods when psychology still needed to gain its territory from pseudo-sciences such as graphology. Perhaps he would have gained an appreciation of the value of interpretative knowledge in psychology, as many nowadays have. In view of his interest in literature and novels, especially the work of James Joyce, it is not impossible that he would have tried to combine a humanist approach to man with an experimental perspective. During the sixties, however, this was not opportune. However idiosyncratic Linschoten may have been, he was part and parcel of the tradition of empirical psychology and believed in the progress of his profession.

9. *Conclusions*

Johannes Linschoten (1925-1964) was one of the best-known phenomenological psychologists in the Netherlands after the Second World War. During the last years of his life -- according to opinion, that is -- he converted to the American experimental psychology which was gaining influence and prestige. This chapter has tried to establish the nature of this "conversion" and to elucidate its background and circumstances.

The following points are of importance:

I

Linschoten's "conversion" does not signify a radical change in his views of phenomenology. He changed his ideas about the methods of research in psychology, which should not proceed phenomenologically-empirically, but empirically-analytically by means of analysis of reality into variables, in order to determine experimental relations between these variables, if possible. With regard to research he rejected phenomenology. On the other hand, he remained confident in phenomenology as a philosophical reflection upon the object and theories of psychology. Thus he also retained a phenomenological critique of the principles of objectifying psychological theories (see point IV, too).

II

The "Utrecht School" was an informal group of traditional scholars whose research was characterized by a philosophical-phenomenological outlook. With the sudden growth of psychology as an academic subject and profession during the fifties, a need developed for a concept of psychology which (a) could be taught to large groups of students; (b) was suitable for practical application to a variety of professions;

(c) would not demand time-consuming philosophical reflection upon social norms and scientific principles. The empirical-analytic psychology which had started to flower in the U.S., seemed to live up to the following promises: clear methods, technical applications, the pretence of being value-free. Thus it grows likely that a young and ambitious professor such as Linschoten adhered to the modern psychology which was gaining ground and rejected the established pre-war philosophical practice of psychology.

III

Linschoten had received phenomenological training from Buytendijk, but also an experimental one which drew him to a psychology based on the ideal of objectivity of the physical sciences. Thus he labored under the prejudice that interpretative disciplines such as the humanities and cultural sciences are, in fact, not true sciences. To the extent that phenomenology resulted in interpretative research, to Linschoten it appeared stained with the odium of subjectivity. It was not truly scientific or, at its best, a preparatory phase of objective investigation. The ideal of objectivity seemed a good criterion to distinguish psychology from non-methodological disciplines and pseudosciences such as graphology.

IV

In the course of his development, Linschoten gradually gains distance from the ahistorical aspects of Husserl's intuition of essences. He arrives at the conclusion that the essence of phenomena does not reside in invariable properties which may be intuited, but should be sought in the variety of examples which have nothing in common except that they belong to a historical process of change. This insight, contained in the philosophies of Wittgenstein, Heidegger, and Gadamer, leads to a form of historical relativism of knowledge. Under the influence of these philosophers, this perspective began penetrating psychology ever since the seventies. In the sixties, however, the scientific climate was not yet ready for heretical ideas of this kind. In his philosophical reflection on the principles of psychology, Linschoten was far ahead of his time. The discrepancy with the developments going on in empirical psychology was so great that he saw no possibility of translating his philosophical ideas into methodological guidelines for an empirical psychology. Hence the split towards the end of his life: advocate of a scientific experimental psychology which considers phenomenology as indispensable and shows the inconceivability of an empirical-analytical (or scientistic) world view.

4

RHETORICAL ANALYSIS AND THE QUESTION OF RELATIVISM: AN EXAMINATION OF THE VIEWS OF KENNETH J. GERGEN

> Here one must realize that complete absence of doubt at some point, even where we would say that 'legitimate' doubt can exist, need not falsify a language-game.
> Wittgenstein, *On Certainty.*

Contents:

1. *Empirical-Analytical versus Interpretative Psychology*

Discussions about psychology's fragmentation and the possibilities for unification and progress often center around the concept of *interpretation.* To suppose that psychological knowledge has interpretative aspects is seen by many as a potential danger for the objective status of the discipline as it is traditionally understood, namely as an empirical-analytical science modelled after the natural sciences. Customarily, the ensuing discussion centers around the question whether psychology has to be strictly regarded as an empirical-analytical science which avoids interpretation, or whether it can or should be conceived as an interpretative or hermeneutical enterprise (cf. Schlenker, 1974).

Interest in this discussion has never waned altogether, although the terms in which these matters are discussed have changed considerably. In this paper, I propose we look at the problem in a somewhat different way. I suggest we look upon the interpretative and the empirical-analytical methods as two equally valid, but different approaches to an understanding of the world. Both of them are perfectly legitimate within the scientific context of studies in the humanities; there are pragmatic and not primarily epistemological reasons on which we decide to use one or the other. Without attempting to list all the good arguments by proponents of interpretative methods in psychology (for example, Gergen 1982; Taylor 1971, Peters 1958), it suffices to say that there are also good reasons to prefer empirical-analytical methods. The question is: do empirical-analytic methods enable researchers to avoid interpretation altogether? As we have seen earlier (see chapter 1, section 11), the answer is an unambiguous but multi-faceted 'no'. Every observation is theory-laden and in that sense it is an interpretation of the world in the light of a theoretical framework (Popper 1959). The positivist myth of neutral data has long been abandoned in philosophy. Science is a rule-governed enterprise, and even methodological rules imply selective and sometimes highly biased points of view. Such selective viewpoints are necessary and need not be regarded as a sign that psychology can no longer be a science or present testable hypotheses. The point is that there are many contacts between viewpoints or values and psychology, so that psychology cannot be regarded as an isolated tower of neutrality (Duintjer 1970). Values are present in every experiment or investigation, as shown, for example, by Morawski & Goldstein (1985) in the case of nuclear war research. Unfortunately, such viewpoints or values usually become clear only when we have the benefit of hindsight. Samelson (1980, 1981) has shown that historical work can be very useful in the critical reflection on psychology. Experimental research and scientific observations -- we come to know about them as a result of all kinds of valuations, cf. Peters & Ceci (1982) -- do not form a foolproof safeguard against subjectivity, rather, they are themselves based on interpretation.

All this does not imply that the empirical-analytical method is basically wrong. The only thing is that it does not provide us with the kind of ideal neutrality that is sometimes taken for granted. As has been argued in chapter 1, working with experimental quantitative methods still obliges one to make value-based decisions and interpret human reality (also see chapter 7). When this fact is not acknowledged, interpretations and decisions are made implicitly and without proper reflection on their importance.

My intention in this chapter is to show that Gergen's work is a reflection on the nature and suppositions of empirical-analytical psychology with its dilemma of interpretations.

2. *Psychology as Rhetoric*

Gergen's reflections emerge from experimental social psychology, which he labels as positivist-empiricist in character. He observes that this kind of science hopes to attain objective and enduring truth or certainty, and is built on the belief in progress through the accumulation of facts. According to Gergen (1980; 1982, ch. 2), there are three assumptions inherent in empiricist social psychology which are untenable. First, there is the assumption of empirical evaluation. Empiricist psychology supposes that a theory may be evaluated against 'the facts', against observations or empirical evidence. Traditionally, theorists maintain that this must result in falsification or confirmation of the theory. Gergen argues that testing in this empiricist sense is impossible in psychology. Due to the interpretative nature of psychological facts, any theory may be related to any set of facts (also see Gergen et al, 1986). What Gergen shows is that the same experimental results may be explained by different theoretical models and these results may also be used as support for virtually any theory. The relationship between theoretical concepts and empirical exemplars is fundamentally ambiguous. It is important to note that all of the examples of the ambiguous nature of facts that Gergen provides stem from social psychology. Second, the empiricist assumes the accumulation of knowledge. However, following the first assumption, namely that the theories are isolated from empirical evidence, the elimination of incorrect theories is impossible in any straightforward way. This means that the chances for progress are very small indeed if one clings to the traditional criterion of verisimilitude. Third, the empiricist assumes that the application of social psychological theories to achieve social good involves prediction and control. But as should be clear from the above, the predictive capabilities of psychological theories are small because predictions are highly ambiguous. Hence, the value of basic theory must be sought in a direction different from prediction and control (Gergen 1980).

However, the foregoing cannot be read as a criticism of empirical psychology. It is a critique of certain assumptions of empiricist psychology. It is *within that framework* that empirical evaluation is impossible or, rather, turns out to be something different from what it is believed to be.

The problems inherent in these three assumptions of empiricist social psychology are illustrated by the so-called interpretative dilemma. Gergen poses this dilemma by describing a situation from everyday life. Ross and Laura approach each other at a social gathering, and Ross reaches out and briefly touches Laura's hair. Precisely what is observed if we see this happen? What action has occurred? How do we normally solve the essential problem of behavioral identification? (Gergen 1980, 1982, 1988). Different interpretations of the action can be given. Indeed it is not easy to say which meaning this action actually has for the participants or for observers. Was the touching of Laura's hair a sign of affection? Or was it an act of derision? It all depends on the context and if we turn for additional information to the retrospective and emergent contexts, we can easily imagine how more and more interpretations become plausible.

Gergen draws three conclusions from this example.

1. The identification of any given action is subject to infinite revision.
2. The anchor point for any given identification is not fundamentally empirical (in the empiricist sense of the word), but relies on a network of interdependent and continuously modifiable interpretations.

3. Any given action may be subject to multiple identifications, no one of which is inherently superior (1980, p. 241; 1982, ch. 2).

If one applies these conclusions to the interpretative basis of social psychology, it becomes clear that the traditional empiricist assumptions are undermined. Gergen concludes that the traditional aims of the discipline must be modified, and sketches the possibilities of social psychology as an interpretative enterprise. In short, instead of describing and explaining a preexisting reality, a theory should be concerned with descriptions of rule systems and conceptual transformations of social life. Common forms of interpretation and their relation to social action might be systematically elucidated. One might also challenge the guiding assumptions of a culture, foster reconsideration of that which is taken for granted, and furnish fresh alternatives for social action. The challenging of common-sense interpretation is what Gergen means by generative theory. Philosophically speaking, we might call this emphasis on the change of common interpretations by means of persuasion a rhetorical position.[1]

In a volume dedicated to social constructionist inquiry (Gergen & Davis 1985), Gergen observes that psychology might look for kinship to the traditional interpretative disciplines. Psychology might gain a lot by developing an affinity with disciplines chiefly concerned with rendering accounts of human meaning systems, for example, literary theory.

Gergen draws an important distinction between two innovations that his alternative conception offers. The first concerns the object of research. This is no longer seen as naturally 'given', but as constituted by social rules and norms. This means that psychology becomes a derivative of social process: "the explanatory locus of human action shifts from the interior region of the mind to the processes and structure of human interchange" (p. 12). The second innovation is on the level of meta-theory. Earlier, Gergen cast doubt on the process of objective warranting. His conclusions also apply to the accounts of social construction. "Such accounts can enable one to escape the confines of the taken for granted. However, the success of such accounts depends primarily on the analyst's capacity to invite, compel, stimulate, or delight the audience, and not on criteria of veracity"

(1985, p. 14). Gergen addresses the possible criticism that such rhetoric may lead to relativism by observing that empiricism does not seem to fare any better in this respect, for the so-called objective foundations of knowledge still have to be justified. But he does acknowledge that " ... constructionism offers no foundational rules of warrant, and in this sense is relativistic. However, this does not mean that 'anything goes'. Because of the inherent dependency of knowledge systems on communities of shared intelligibility, scientific activity will always be governed in large measure by normative rules" (p. 14).

In a paper called "If Persons Are Texts", Gergen (1988) addresses the question how his rhetorical position relates to the hermeneutic approach in psychology. Hermeneutics, generally connected with the work of the German philosopher H.G. Gadamer, maintains that there is at least one legitimate alternative to the scientific methodical approach to reality. The interpretative approach used in the cultural and historical disciplines is not methodical in empirical-analytical terms, but it nevertheless leads to empirical knowledge. This interpretative kind of knowledge is not arbitrary and is open to validation. However, its character is historical which means that it is part of 'effective history' (*Wirkungsgeschichte*) in the sense that later generations may judge differently from their vantage points. Not only does knowledge change, but *the standards* change with which knowledge is evaluated. Gadamer seems to be ambiguous as to the question of progress in the hermeneutical disciplines; sometimes he suggests that a new understanding implies a better understanding, in other contexts he calls it a 'different understanding'.

As a rhetorician, Gergen is more inclined to challenging existing forms of understanding and to analyze the way persuasion works. As we have seen above, he casts doubt on the notion of a 'correct' interpretation or 'the best' interpretation. Similarly, he cannot accept the common understanding by the 'hermeneuticists' of Gadamer's position. Gergen prefers the ideas of "literary theorists in general" and "deconstructionists in particular" (1988, p. 43). In literary theory, the reader has displaced the text as the center of concern. However, the ensuing deconstruction of the text and its author leaves us with another impasse. It seems that human understanding is impossible. To quote Gergen again: "In the process of reading, both the text and its author are obliterated. The individual again falls back into isolation, unable to know, and unable to communicate" (p. 44). In reaction to these problems, Gergen sketches an alternative for the metaphor of a person as text. His alternative rests on the assumptions that (a) the dualism between interior and exterior must be abandoned. Human actions are what they are -- we can only confront each others actions directly, and (b) the words of others are of significant consequence to our actions; we are not self-contained monads.

This last move is puzzling. It seems that Gergen falls back on what seems to be, essentially, Gadamer's position. Gadamer can certainly not be accused of being a dualist of exterior (actions) and interior (intentions). Intentions are irrelevant and futile to Gadamer and never play a role in interpretation. Further, he acknowledges the necessity of interpreting in those cases where a natural direct understanding is impossible: for example, the reading of an ancient text, or the understanding of a culture different from our own. Even then, we can confront the others actions directly, or approach the text directly in the hermeneutic circle. Indeed, in the process of following the hermeneutic circle, the words of the object are of significant consequence for our actions. Our own preconceptions are brought into play. The horizon of the interpreter's understanding is affected by reading the text. When we reach a fusion of the horizons of understanding -- even in the process of reading a text -- it is hardly possible to view the reader or interlocutor as a 'self-contained monad', to use Gergen's terms. It seems that Gergen unwittingly moves back into the realm of Gadamerian hermeneutics. Certain formulations which he uses at the end of the article form evidence for this surmise.

For example, he writes that "the meanings of words, gestures, or actions are realized within the unfolding patterns of relationship" (1988, p. 46). We may look, not inward, "but outward into the continuously expanding horizon of the relationship" (ibid). Gergen mentions the expression of depression as an example. "As our participants showed us, there are only a limited set of discursive moves that may be made" (p. 48). Following this new metaphor of the game, the dance, or the relationship, we may explore the embedding of relational scenarios. "Rather than exploring the unknown world of the interior, one moves to the level of client-therapist relationship" (p. 49). "Questions of validity are replaced by queries into the forms of relatedness into which our verbal expressions (among others) fall, and into their implications and alternatives" (p. 50).

These quotations show that there is at least one recurring theme in Gergen's work: the opposition between validity, truth, objectivity, and stable insight on the one hand, and changing meanings, developing insights, open-ended interpretations, and relative truth on the other. Let us now have a closer look at some philosophical presuppositions of this theme and the rhetorical position in general.

3. *An Evaluation of the Rhetorical Position*

Earlier, I called Gergen's conception of the foundations and nature of psychology a rhetorical conception of social psychology. It is not surprising that various forms of criticism have been raised against these ideas, because they run counter to established psychological theorizing. Gergen so strongly denies the possibility of objective knowledge, that his ideas become a threat for the very enterprise of (social) psychology. While I would maintain that this is not a necessary conclusion from his rhetorical position, there are aspects in Gergen's writings which invite this reading. Let me try to elucidate the discussion by raising three questions in connection with the evaluation of the rhetorical conception of social psychology.

1. Gergen views the interpretation of human action as essentially ungrounded and open to infinite revision. But is this view not premised on a misconceived dilemma: either there are rational foundations, or there are no foundations at all? My contention is that most of the interpretations we give are not rationally justified in the sense required by strict empiricism, but still they are not arbitrary or subjective because they are based on the practice of our form of life (i.e. culture or scientific paradigm).
2. The contextual validation of interpretations of human action is regarded by Gergen as essentially impossible. The problems of

evaluating theories and interpretations in the context of empirical-analytical research are convincingly posed. However, is the endless revision of interpretations, as Gergen describes it, also possible in the context of everyday life, and even if it is possible, does it constitute an actual problem for a discipline that does not work on empiricist assumptions? It seems that traditional interpretative disciplines have found ways to deal adequately with the evaluation of interpretative theories.

3. Gergen has formulated an alternative aim for social psychology. In this rhetorical conception, psychology must provide alternatives for common forms of understanding, and form a generative theory. However, can these alternative aims not be seen as an enrichment of empirical-analytical and interpretative psychologies, instead of as an antidote? Empirical research could be part of the rhetorical task. I will come back to this point in chapters 6 and 7.

4. *The Basis of Knowledge*

The idea that knowledge has certain and rational foundations has been gradually undermined in this century. Generally, philosophers do not believe that a complete justification of knowledge claims is possible. Let me review some important lines of development.

Popper (1959/1934) was first in demonstrating that the logical positivists' claim that scientific knowledge rests on certain foundations was unwarranted. Popper posited a conventional basis for our knowledge claims. Scientific knowledge rests on basic propositions. However, testing is always possible and offers a guarantee against dogmatism. The character of scientific knowledge is that it cannot be justified by reference to indubitable facts. Rather, it may be corroborated by tests; testability is the criterion for science.

About thirty years later, Thomas Kuhn (1962) radicalized the fasificationist ideas about the foundations and the development of scientific theories. According to Kuhn, the nature of the scientific basis has traditionally been misunderstood. This basis of science is not propositional, but it consists of exemplars of good research. As a last resort, a scientist is not able to justify his theories with the help of knowledge claims or methodological rules: he must refer to paradigms of what counts in his science as sound research (Cf. Wittgenstein 1969, 139). On this account, knowledge is further undermined, or better still relativized: knowledge and rationality are valid concepts when measured against the standards of a certain paradigm or disciplinary matrix.

Kuhn's ideas were clearly inspired by the later Wittgenstein. In *Philosophical Investigations* (1953) and *On Certainty* (1969), Wittgenstein addresses the philosophical problem of the foundations of knowledge. He stresses the imbeddedness of all our knowledge in language games and, eventually, forms of life. His analysis of rule-following behavior demonstrates that rules alone are not sufficient to guide human action. In the end, justification is impossible and we act without rational grounds, but with certainty. Wittgenstein also shows that every application of a rule involves a decision. He imagines a case where a student fails to continue a number series in the way we expect. However, we are unable to convince him on the basis of rational arguments that he is wrong. Instead we become involved in a fruitless discussion about the concept of 'sameness', and in the end we are forced to admit that something is right "because we all do it". (Wittgenstein 1953, 186: "It would almost be more correct to say, not that an intuition was needed at every stage, but that a new decision was needed at every stage.")

In *On Certainty*, Wittgenstein is even clearer in this respect: "Giving grounds, however, justifying the evidence, comes to an end;- but the end is not certain propositions striking us immediately as true, i.e. it is not a kind of *seeing* on our part; it is our *acting*, which lies at the bottom of the language game" (Wittgenstein 1969, 204). We may distinguish these practical certainties in our forms of life from the more reflexive certainties we entertain. The concept of certainty is a second and related way in which Wittgenstein indicates the nature of the basis of our knowledge. Knowledge and certainty form mutually exclusive categories for him. If we know something, we are able to present evidence and grounds for it, and so we are not certain. But if we are certain (for example, that these are real human people who are sitting in front of me), we are not able to state the reasons for our belief, nor are we generally able to doubt. "If you tried to doubt everything you would not get as far as doubting anything. The game of doubting itself presupposes certainty" (Wittgenstein 1969, 115; cf. 120, 370, 391).

What implications might these philosophical analyses have for the rhetorical position? I believe that Wittgenstein convincingly shows the non-rational, but nevertheless indubitable foundations of human knowledge. Normally we accept these foundations; only in exceptional cases are we willing and able to doubt. When Gergen points to the lack of rational foundations for our everyday interpretations, he is entirely right. But this does not open the door to unlimited doubt and continuous revision of all our interpretations. Though some revisions are possible in principle, they would only actually occur in exceptional cases. Not some rational foundation, but only the traditional practices and a system of certainties present in every human culture provide safeguards against subjectivity and arbitrariness in interpretation.

5. *The Revision of Interpretations*

In Gergen's view, the context of an action does not help us in determining the meaning of an action. The example of Ross and Laura shows that enlarging the context only tends to complicate the interpretation: more information about the context tends to create more possibilities of interpretation.

However, the example must not blind us to the innumerable situations in everyday life where we directly perceive the meaning of actions. And if it is not a case of unproblematic perception, we usually find out in conversation what is at stake. Problems of interpretation should not be denied, but they must be properly situated in a Wittgensteinian manner as exceptions against the backdrop of reasonably well-ordered language games of everyday life.

There is one special situation which artificially creates problems in interpretation: the psychological experiment. Usually the normal context is removed and subjects are asked to react to certain contrived manipulations. Here, indeed, it is very difficult to say what the resulting responses mean (cf. Gergen 1978). It is significant that Gergen only takes one example from everyday life as evidence for his thesis that interpretations are open to infinite revision. And one wonders whether the problems of Laura and Ross occur with regularity in daily life. The rest of Gergen's evidence is taken from the field of social psychology, and it tells us more about the difficulties inherent in empiricist research than it does about interpretations of action in natural contexts (cf. Brandt 1982).

6. *Generative Theory: Psychology as Rhetoric*

In the analysis of mainstream social psychology, it becomes clear that investigations which fail to challenge common-sense knowledge in our culture are not so easily challenged by alternative explanations of the results. This leads to conservatism: "the review process ensures that the scientific literature will not deviate markedly from 'what every reasonable person' already knows" (Gergen 1980, p. 254). This is certainly a good reason for propagating audacious theorizing. But does rhetorical analysis exclude all kinds of explanatory and interpretative understanding of existing norms, rules, and forms of action? Confronted with empiricist defenders of neutrality, it seems necessary to stress the variable and continuously changing nature of human reality. But these changes take place against a massive background of continuity -- also in the cultural domain. It seems that one cannot even tell whether certain norms are right or wrong, desirable or undesirable, without studying and interpreting actual language games. The emphasis on the flexible character of interpretation and the aim of audacious theorizing may be seen as useful antidotes against empirical-analytical dogmatism, but these need not become values in themselves. If they do, they must be deconstructed in turn (Carveth, 1984).

7. *Does Rhetorical Analysis Lead to Relativism?*

The tendency in Gergen's work to stress the infinite diversity of human behavior and to deny the possibility of discovering regularities by means of more traditional research is criticized by Jahoda (1986).

Jahoda argues that the conception of man as free and autonomous is also a typical Western ideal. Of course this is a legitimate value to defend, also when it is a basis for theorizing. In part, Gergen's emphasis on freedom can be ascribed to the fact that he is in constant discussion with his empiricist opponents. For after all, it is empiricist metatheory which has as its aim timeless truths and general laws, but has produced only limited knowledge of a reduced reality heavily impregnated by temporary norms.

However, the radical move to the opposite position, namely that psychology must not aim at the truth, must not seek validation for its knowledge claims and must restrict itself to persuasion, seems somewhat too simple. When Gergen says: "the success of such accounts [of social construction] depends primarily on the analyst's capacity to invite, compel, stimulate, or delight the audience, and not on criteria of veracity" (Gergen 1985a, p. 14), I think he creates a contrast which is not based on a real opposition. The audience within psychology is only compelled or stimulated by work which meets certain criteria of veracity. This veracity has nothing to do with old-fashioned ideas about transhistorical truths or absolute justification for knowledge. Relativism is inevitable in the sense that historical evolution might change the standards with which scientific knowledge is evaluated. Also, psychological knowledge can be seen from different vantage points: there is more than one theoretical value orientation. It is not always possible to reach an intersubjective judgment about certain matters. These are restrictions which must be kept in mind when one defends a claim to knowledge. Nevertheless, accepting limits to our knowledge does not prevent us from believing that we are searching for the truth. This is a simple distinction between different levels of discourse: within science we aim for the best interpretations possible with respect to truth, veracity, relevance. But taking the vantage point of the philosopher, and reflecting upon science, we realize that the knowledge acquired does not transcend our historical and cultural limitations. Rhetorical analysis aims to show the fluctuating character of reality. In this process, fixed meanings are deconstructed. Yet, even when rhetoricians deconstruct their own positions, they claim to be truthful about reality, to reveal important aspects of reality. In this sense, empirical-analytical psychology, hermeneutics, and rhetoric share an important goal, that is, they all aim for the truth. In his critiques of the assumptions of empiricist psychology, Gergen has demonstrated that the empirical-analytical method presents us with psychological knowledge that is dependent upon the cultural and historical context. The same holds true for his rhetorical conception. The conclusion may sound paradoxical: in his radical rejection of the aims of empiricist psychology, Gergen remains entangled in one central presupposition of the empirical-analytical world view. He assumes that apart from the realm of natural science, no real knowledge can be found, and that any pursuit of truth in the humanities is futile. However, this presupposition rests on a shaky basis indeed.

8. *Alternatives for the Acceptance of Relativism*

How valid is the hypothesis that interpretative research leads to inherently subjective results? The literature, both within and without the field of psychology, presents a variety of arguments that undermine this conception of interpretation. Runyan (1982) has pointed out that even where a variety of plausible interpretations could be given, a critical assessment of the evidence presented is crucial. We may encounter such a plethora of interpretations in clinical studies (Fosshage & Loew, 1978; cf. this volume, chapter 7), in psychobiography (Runyan, 1982), in history and traditional philology (Oudemans & Lardinois, 1987), and in cognitive psychology (Erdelyi, 1985). The authors mentioned all share the belief that the pursuit of knowledge and truth is essential in such studies. Some provide rules and methods for sound interpretative work (French & Fromm, 1964), while others stress the fact that interpretations ought to be tested against evidence (Erdelyi, 1985; Runyan, 1982). Some warn against the quantitative methodological imperative in psychology (Danziger, 1985a); others reject empirical-analytical thought as a world view (De Boer, 1983b; see Linschoten's arguments as presented in chapter 3 of this volume). Interpretative disciplines may offer us real knowledge, though a different kind of knowledge than many psychologists would expect.

5

THE HERMENEUTICAL CONCEPTION OF PSYCHOANALYSIS: GRÜNBAUM'S *FOUNDATIONS OF PSYCHOANALYSIS*

Contents:

1. *Introduction*

Since 1976, Adolf Grünbaum has published a series of articles on the philosophy of psychoanalysis; in 1984 they were collected in his book *The Foundations of Psychoanalysis*. Grünbaum is first of all concerned with the question of whether psychoanalysis is a science. Secondly, he is trying to show that the inductivist criteria for science which he favors may be fruitfully applied to psychoanalysis. Put very briefly, his conclusions are that Freud's psychoanalytic theory is scientific (contrary to Popper's claim) but that, alas, empirical evidence to support its truth is still lacking at this moment. In a lengthy introduction to the book (94 pages), Grünbaum criticizes another conception of the nature of psychoanalytic theory, that is, the hermeneutic interpretation of psychoanalysis.

The aim of this chapter is to show that Grünbaum's critique of the hermeneutical conception rests on basic misunderstandings and very significant errors in interpretation. For brevity's sake, consideration will be restricted to Grünbaum's treatment of Jürgen Habermas's ideas, but examination of Grünbaum's criticisms of Paul Ricoeur, a second representative of the hermeneutic enterprise, would lead to similar conclusions. The author's position will be that Grünbaum's evaluation of Freud's theory is only valid when one starts from a narrow absolutist conception of empirical-analytical science, and believes that there is only one legitimate form of knowledge: namely, deductive-nomological explanations. An alternative conception of psychoanalysis will be outlined.

2. *The Empirical-Analytical Conception of Science*

Let us start by making clear what we understand the empirical-analytical method to be (De Boer, 1983a). It is designed to:

1. Provide descriptions by analyzing reality into independent variables; and
2. Find laws connecting these variables, or at least statistical regularities in their interaction.

In this way, it becomes possible to provide deductive-nomological explanations.

The author believes that no additional assumptions are necessary. For example, empirical-analytical science does not have to restrict itself to material phenomena. In this respect we whole-heartedly agree with Adolf Grünbaum when he emphatically declares: "the causal relevance is a matter of whether X -- be it physical, mental or psycho-physical -- MAKES A DIFFERENCE to the occurrence of Y, or AFFECTS THE INCIDENCE of Y" (Grünbaum, 1984, p. 72). But whereas the variable X may be ontologically neutral in the way stated here, the presuppositions (or postulates) of empirical-analytical science are not. Many philosophers believe that reality, and especially human and cultural reality, is structured by internal relations, and may only secondarily be perceived as consisting of logically independent facts connected by laws. Indeed, we may approach the human and cultural world with the empirical-analytical method, but that is only one of the possible approaches. When the social sciences use that approach, they view the human world as a complex concatenation of logically independent facts with lawlike connections. This picture may enlighten certain facets of the world and may ideally result in possibilities of prediction and control of human affairs. In other respects it distorts our normal picture of reality or it does not fit into our everyday expectations. In any case, we are not forced to accept it and may find traditional common-sense notions about reality easier to live with. In daily life it seems advisable to use a non-atomistic view of the world because it makes dealing with our fellow beings easier. In the domain of scientific research, however, empirical-analytical thinking may be valuable.

The relative status of the empirical-analytical approach may be elucidated by pointing out the fact that scientific thinking is metaphorical. The use of metaphor may be defined as the application of descriptive terms to objects to which they are imaginatively but not literally applicable (Carveth, 1984). We may in some circumstances fruitfully apply a certain class of concepts, but we may also use other metaphors.

The use of metaphors changes, of course. In some parts of science once-popular metaphors have lost their creative new function and "died". Many scientists never even realize they use them persistently. The hermeneutical disciplines try to formulate alternatives: Here one aims to generate different metaphors, each aiming in its own way to give a vision of reality. (Cf. Gergen's (1982) notion of 'generative theory'). For example, human reality may be seen as a meaningful text which is able to tell us something, which may be understood and may even be true.

To recapitulate, empirical-analytical science tries to analyze reality into independent variables and to find the laws connecting these variables. It acts on the assumptions (1) that such an analysis is possible without serious distortion of reality, and (2) that reality is determined by laws. This is one of the possible ways to approach reality. To say that it forms the only approach possible is to make an ontological claim. While the empirical-analytical approach encourages metaphors such as "the mind is a computer", "human memory is a hologram", and "the ego is a brittle object", it excludes another class of metaphors as being unsuitable for scientific goals, for example, "human life is a text".

Many philosophers of science would not accept the relativism implied by a recognition of the hermeneutical approach. They would argue that the empirical-analytical method is a superior approach to reality, and the only way to obtain objective knowledge. Applied to psychoanalysis, this means that the value of a hermeneutical conception of either theory or practice would be denied. Such a conception is equated with subjectivity and arbitrariness. In this context Blight (1981) remarks, for example, "To anyone whose views derive from a more or less empiricist tradition, this may well be the central paradox, and hence stumbling block, of the hermeneutical program: logic and truth itself become, if not quite arbitrary, at least plastic, perhaps infinitely so" (p. 167).

Eagle (1980) argues that psychoanalysis needs more than common sense motivational explanation alone and that, given the fact that it provides a therapeutical treatment, "there is simply no way that psychoanalysis can shrug off problems of accountability - which, after all, is the pragmatic side of reliability and validity - and there is no way, I believe, that psychoanalysis can legitimately and comfortably content itself simply with the status of a hermeneutic endeavor" (pp. 376-377).

These authors join Grünbaum in making an important contrast, with far-reaching consequences: on the one side, scientific knowledge, on the other side, purely arbitrary statements, not even deserving the title of "knowledge". This involves a kind of splitting off: the two things are not relatively distinct from one another, but absolutely antithetical. The author believes that this contrast rests on the belief in an ontological and epistemological claim which must be supported by philosophical arguments, even when its truth may seem evident in certain circles.

3. *Abraham Anton Grünbaum's Critique of Psychoanalysis*

The conflict between empirical-analytical and hermeneutical approaches in psychoanalysis has led to an interesting variety of interpretations of this discipline. In mainstream psychoanalytic thinking, two opinions are generally found:

1. What analysts do in their therapies is to interpret verbal utterances, symptoms, dreams, parapraxes, and actions (Van Leeuwen, 1973).
2. Psychoanalytic metatheory depicts the theory, following Freud in his theoretical reflections, as a natural science, aiming at deductive-nomological explanations.

For those believing that the process of interpretation starts from assumptions very unlike those of empirical-analytical science, there is a tension between (1) and (2). Indeed, a strong case can be made to the effect that interpretation cannot be analyzed as subsuming particular cases under general laws (Von Wright 1971, Van Leeuwen, 1973). One way out of the dilemma is to say that traditional psychoanalytic metatheory was mistaken, as was Freud. For many analysts and philosophers this is not an attractive solution: they try to show that (1) and (2) are compatible because the interpretation of meaning must always be open for corroboration in suggesting an underlying causal explanation. The analyst interprets a lapse, say a man's forgetting of the Latin pronoun, *aliquis*, by referring to his repressed fear of making his womanfriend pregnant. At the same time, as Freud argued, a causal explanation may be provided: the act of forgetting is the result of previous occurrences, among which is an act of repression (Freud, 1901b, chapter 2; Grünbaum, 1984, pp. 58-59).

Once psychoanalysis is considered to be an empirical-analytical science, it must, of course, be judged by the standards of this type of science, and as the reader may know, usually one of two verdicts results from the ensuing evaluation: psychoanalysis is unscientific (Popper) or psychoanalysis is scientific but there is no adequate evidence to corroborate its hypothesized causal explanations.

Grünbaum defends the latter position. In interesting parts of his book he shows that Popper's still fashionable theses about the unfalsifiability of psychoanalysis are not based on a serious reading of Freud and must be considered refuted (1984, chapter 11).[1] Of course, there are psychoanalysts who try to escape these problems by maintaining that at the moment there is at least some supporting empirical evidence available, while more research efforts must provide the required extra confirmations. But why should we not refuse to accept the scientific standards issuing from a metaphor which is powerful but, as argued, has only a relative right of existence? The philosopher A.A. Grünbaum was among the first to draw this conclusion.

In order to avoid confusion arising from the introduction of a second Grünbaum on the scene, it should be noted that Abraham Anton Grünbaum was born in Odessa in 1885, received his training as a philosopher and an experimental psychologist with Wundt in Leipzig, wrote his dissertation under Külpe in Würzburg, and thereafter held positions at the universities of Utrecht and Amsterdam between World War I and II. He died in 1932.

One of his few publications that deal with psychoanalysis is "Die Idee der Psychoanalyse und die Erkenntnistheorie" (Grünbaum, 1928). This article contains ideas which are still remarkably fresh and anticipates currently fashionable hermeneutic interpretations of psychoanalysis. A.A. Grünbaum points to three peculiar traits of psychoanalysis which do not fit into Freud's image of it as a natural science.

1. There is Freud's strange assertion that only those who have been in training analysis have developed the capacities necessary to discuss psychoanalytic matters (Freud, 1926e, p. 199). A.A. Grünbaum (1928) describes this as "the correct, but not fully understood insight that psychoanalysis is not a science... Knowledge is at the same time a practical, active experience of the whole, concrete situation... The practical therapy is an essential influence on the theory... by its situational character as *active knowledge by two*" (pp. 205-206).[2]

Even if the training analysis would become optional, and psychoanalytic organizations would restrict themselves to a kind of advice for candidates that ideally an analyst should have undergone psychoanalysis himself (Bernfeld, 1962), it would remain a phenomenon unique to psychoanalysis, unheard of in both the empirical-analytical and the hermeneutical disciplines. Although a knowledge of chemistry entails an understanding of the laboratory procedures whereby chemists carry on their investigations, the chemist is not required to reflect on his own personality. Analogously, as Freud (1937a) says, "nobody maintains that a physician is incapable of treating internal diseases if his own internal organs are not sound ..." (p. 247).

For the analyst, on the other hand, it is not sufficient to standardize himself as an instrument of measurement, as Savodnik (1976) would have it. It is not a matter of calibration, but a controlled employment of his own feelings in the (counter-)transference situation. In hermeneutical disciplines, only a partial parallel can be found, for example, when Gadamer (1960) requires that the interpreter brings his preconceived opinions *(Vorurteile)* into play and has an attitude of openness for the different opinions of the other (a partner in a dialogue, or a text) during the process of interpretation.

2. Secondly, A. A. Grünbaum contends: "psychoanalysis -- it is part of the fascination it has for us -- wishes to shed light on the concrete, individual aspects of reality" (1928, p. 206). Paradoxically, science in general is not really interested in reality in its concreteness; it is interested in laws. "Psychoanalysis, with its ideal ... of psychical determinism, wants to proceed, not from reality to rules, but the other way round, from the rule to the reality of the individual case, to express and do justice to its whole quantitative variety ... When psychoanalysis does not go into detail, it is considered boring and justly so" (pp. 206-207). Indeed, psychoanalytic explanations are often considered schematic and monotonous. The same reproach is never made against scientific explanations, though they always contain the same categories and concepts. When different standards are used in the evaluation of psychoanalysis, this might be considered as evidence for its different character: it aims to capture the meaning of individual traits and occurrences, and is actually not scientific explanation, but interpretation.

Psychoanalysis is not interested in quantitative (external) covariations, but in meaning relations. "In scientific terms, 'just' interpreting would be an inferior method; for psychoanalysis, it is the main constituent of its procedure" (1928, p. 208).

3. A third peculiarity of psychoanalysis, A.A. Grünbaum explains, is given in the influence Freud's ideas exert on the common sense perception of mental life. We perceive psychological reality in a different way since Freud; psychoanalytical hypotheses have become

common sense. One is tempted to object here that the same could be said of hypotheses from the natural sciences. But this is only partially true: we still watch sunsets with the idea that the sun sinks, whereas Grünbaum has no trouble indicating several points where psychoanalysis penetrates daily life. The psyche is goal-directed, it contains ambivalent instincts; psychological reality is partly unconscious and may be interpreted in accordance with analytical maxims. All these insights gradually constitute psychological knowledge. Psychoanalytical knowledge will some day be the a priori of any psychological theory. "And so, the psychoanalytical type of knowledge nowadays starts to penetrate the characteristics of the psyche itself. The epistemology of psychology -- which is not yet written -- will partly have to be a theory of mind as transformed by psychoanalysis" (Grünbaum, 1928, p. 211).

4. *Habermas's Conception of Psychoanalysis*

Adolf Grünbaum (1984) rejects the hermeneutic conception of psychoanalysis in the first part of his book. He argues against the positions of Jürgen Habermas, Paul Ricoeur, and the late George Klein. This discussion, however, as noted earlier, will be restricted to his arguments against Habermas's position.

The first question we must ask is, what did Habermas really say? The impression created by Adolf Grünbaum is so misleading that a recapitulation of Habermas's main theses is necessary. Put briefly, Habermas regards psychoanalysis as a discipline in which causal connections are formulated hypothetically as hermeneutically understandable meaning structures. Knowledge about these connections is not used to manipulatively transform a given situation, but to start a process of self-reflection.

The patient is an active participant in the search for his or her idiographic life history. The analyst is not looking for regularities in the patient's behavior with the aim of using them for control or prediction of the patient's future behavior; the real aim is to interpret all unexpected expressions on the patient's part as constituents of a highly individual life history. The analysis is completed when the narration is complete, that is to say, when the patient is able to tell his own story without "gaps". Habermas contrasts general theories with general interpretations. General theories are found in the empirical-analytical sciences. They explain phenomena by subsuming them under laws and so they may be tested in experiments. The clinical theory of psychoanalysis, on the other hand, consists of general interpretations which function as schemata or heuristic devices to interpret individual life histories. Metapsychology forms the framework in which these general interpretations are formulated. The interpretative schemata form the background for the strictly individual narration created in every particular analysis. General interpretations have three peculiar characteristics which make them quite different from general theories, according to Habermas.

1. The general interpretation is a narration put in *ordinary language*. A typical life history containing anonymous roles and schemata of interaction is to be converted into an individual history in the course of an analysis. Psychoanalysis is the study of the idiographic, the concrete, individual life history.

2. The second characteristic concerns the validation of general interpretations. The analyst suggests an interpretation or construction on the basis of the story told by the analysand; a story which is typically interlaced with gaps, symptoms, dreams, and lapses. The analysand may reply with a *yes*: I believe this is true -- or a *no*; but given his assumption of the unconscious, it is not surprising that Freud attaches little importance to such an utterance in itself. *Yes* may mean a wish to please the analyst, *no* could be a sign of resistance. Habermas agrees with Freud that these answers are not decisive for the truth of the interpretation, because they must be interpreted. More important information is gathered by observing the direction in which the analysis proceeds from now on. Does the analysand react with spontaneous free associations, memories, and so on? Only such reactions, in the context of the subsequent development of the analysis, may be interpreted as experiences of self-reflection, and for that matter, as corroborations of the interpretation. Habermas repeatedly stresses this point: "Freud is right in insisting that only the further course of analysis can decide a construction's usefulness or

lack of it. Only the context of the self-formative process as a whole has confirming and falsifying power" (Habermas 1978, p. 269). This is the "dimension of self-reflection" which characterizes general interpretation, according to Habermas.

3. The third characteristic of general interpretations concerns the logic of explanation. General interpretations form a mixed discourse of hermeneutical interpretation and causal explanation. Between the repressed trauma (or fantasy about a trauma) and the later symptoms, a kind of causality may be discovered. This so-called "causality of fate" may be affected by a therapy through a process of self-reflection: the repression may be overcome, the symptoms made to vanish. The lawlike connection between certain situations and stereotyped reactions of the individual turns out to be a "pseudolaw" when an analysand discovers that it has the character of a meaning relation which may be changed. Thus general interpretations balance on the boundary between two very different language games: (a) a language in which free choice, purposive action, social rules, and responsibility are central concepts; and (b) a language in which human behavior is described in terms of mere regularities, mechanisms, and laws. According to Habermas, psychoanalysis asks the patient to take responsibility for his own behavior, even where it seems to be meaningless and not purposive. Gradually, the patient's behavior may then change its character in the direction of language game (a).[3] This is not to say of course that laws are changed by self-reflection. Only their domain of application is made smaller; certain initial conditions no longer apply.

As Habermas puts it clearly in the appendix to *Knowledge and Human Interests* (an article which first appeared in German in 1965): "[psychoanalysis takes into account that] information about lawlike connections sets off a process of reflection in the consciousness of those whom the laws are about. Thus the level of unreflected consciousness, which is one of the initial conditions of such laws, can be transformed. Of course, to this end a critically mediated knowledge of laws cannot through reflection alone render a law itself inoperative, but it can render it inapplicable" (Habermas 1978, p. 310). Or, put in slightly different terms: "The causal connection between the original scene, defense and symptom is not anchored in the invariance of nature according to natural laws but only in the spontaneously generated invariance of life history by the repetition compulsion, which can nevertheless be dissolved by the power of reflection" (p. 271).

In short, Habermas maintains that the invariance of a *life history* may be influenced by self-reflection. A repetition compulsion, for example, is pseudo-lawlike: under certain circumstances it allows us to make predictions. But such a "law" ceases to determine the individual's behavior once a relevant repression is overcome. External relations between occurrences are interpreted as potentially meaningful relations for the patient. The reported reason, ascribed to a third person, may become the "stated reason" which he himself gives (Toulmin, 1954); then the individual is able to make this own choice: does he consider his own reason good enough to motivate his traditional behavior?

5. *Grünbaum's Repudiation of the Hermeneutic Conception of Psychoanalysis*

The reader of *Knowledge and Human Interests* (1978) who turns to Grünbaum's comments on this book may very well form the idea that Grünbaum is speaking about another work or commenting on a different author. This may be explained by the fact that Grünbaum not only prefers a certain ontological position - the idea that empirical-analytical science provides a universal method - but also denies the rationality of all other positions. No discussion with philosophers of different persuasions seems to be possible because, one after another, they are dismissed as irrational.

Taking this into account, it is admirable that Grünbaum managed to read at least parts of Habermas's work, because to him the astrology column of *Cosmopolitan* must be an oasis of sound judgment and rational persuasion compared with chapters 10 and 11 of *Knowledge and Human Interests*. This, at least, is the impression that one gains from the introduction to *The Foundations of Psychoanalysis*. "Habermas has treated us to a procession of logical enormities interlaced with homiletic *ipse dixits*", as Grünbaum cries out despairingly on page 42.

Grünbaum's objections to Habermas are presented in four separate points:

1. It is impossible to overcome laws, as Habermas holds (Grünbaum, 1984, pp. 9-15).

2. Habermas seriously misconstrues natural science when he maintains that explanations in the natural sciences are ahistorical. Habermas's example of what subsuming under a law in the natural sciences involves is too simple: "this stone" is considered, for example, as "mass" (1984, pp. 15-21). Also, Grünbaum contends, Habermas seems to believe that instant falsification of a hypothesis in the natural sciences is possible. Apparently, he has never heard of Duhem's (1954) insight that the presence of background knowledge is a complicating factor in interpreting the results of a test (pp. 35-36).

3. Habermas, Grünbaum contends, holds the absurd opinion that patients have privileged cognitive access in relation to the validation of psychoanalytic hypotheses. The patient is the "ultimate arbiter", as Habermas would have it (1984, pp. 21-43).

4. Habermas "contrived the exegetical myth", according to Grünbaum, "that the mature Freud had deemed the metapsychology primordially scientific on ontological grounds" (1984, p. 84). Habermas would maintain, moreover, that "Freud's attribution of scientificity to the clinical theory is a *misextrapolation* from the primordially scientific metapsychology" (p. 84). Grünbaum then argues that Freud's criterion of scientificity was actually not ontologically reductive, but methodological or epistemic. Consequently, he claimed natural science status first and foremost for his clinical theory, whereupon his metapsychology was built as a theoretical, partly speculative superstructure.

Some of these arguments may be dismissed easily, because they appear to be based upon misreadings and serious misconstructions of what Habermas says.

1. We saw earlier that Habermas (1978) is perfectly aware that laws cannot be changed by human will, nor by self-reflection (see above, p. 102).

2. Also, Habermas would agree with Grünbaum (1984) and Duhem

(1954) that falsification is only possible presuming the truth of all background knowledge involved. Indeed, Habermas never argues that this is a point of difference between natural science and psychoanalysis, as Grünbaum suggests (1984, pp. 35-36). Nor will it serve Grünbaum to deny differences between natural sciences and psychoanalysis by arguing that natural science explanation is sometimes historical (pp. 15-20) and sometimes interpretative, (pp. 90-91). The important difference is that historians try to understand unique events, and the narrative explanations given can never be validated by testing the laws involved. Historians could argue, hermeneutically, that they use other means of validation in their discipline.[4]

But the position of the interpreter is also historical in an important sense: the interpreter is a partner in a dialogue and knows that his interpretation is also determined by his own position in history. History must be rewritten continuously as times change. The same applies to the individual life history reconstructed in psychoanalysis (Spence, 1983).

3. Grünbaum spends 20 pages arguing that it is absurd to presuppose that the patient has privileged cognitive access to the truth of the construction offered to him by the analyst (1984, pp. 21-43). The ingenuity of his reasoning is ill-addressed, however, as Habermas holds no such opinion. Indeed, Habermas (1978) maintains that the validity of general interpretations depends "on the accomplishment of self-reflection and subsequent communication between the investigator and his 'object' " (p. 261). With "self-reflection", however, he doesn't refer to a private insight which enables the patient to decide about the correctness of the constructions and interpretations offered to him by the analyst. We have seen already that neither Freud nor Habermas attaches much importance to the first reaction of the patient in response to an analytic interpretation. The validity of the interpretation is inferred from the reactions, implicitly or explicitly made by the patient, in the total context of the analysis. How does the analysis proceed from the moment the interpretation is made? Are free associations or new memories produced which may serve as a confirmation of the adequacy of the construction? Alternatively, if no memories come to light after a certain period of

time, is the process of self-reflection proceeding smoothly while the patient is convinced of the truth of the construction?

In that case, as Freud (1937b) maintains in his well-known paper on constructions, a conviction may perform the same function as real memories; we have not got a reconstruction, but a construction. Here again, the way in which the individual reacts to the construction is crucial. Is he convinced? Then the construction may be true. Will he never be convinced? Then the construction might still be true, but this is undecidable. Grünbaum (1984) mistakenly assumes that the patient's response is no longer important in the latter case, when no confirmative memories are produced (pp. 32-33).

4. Habermas's line of reasoning concerning Freud's scientific self-misunderstanding consists of the following steps.

a. Freud's first level of observation and evidence is the level of clinical interpretation.

b. Then Freud starts theorizing on this basis. A theoretical superstructure comes into being: the speculative metapsychology.

c. Satisfied with his new concepts and explanatory hypotheses, Freud subsequently tries to describe clinical phenomena in metapsychological language.

However, clinical phenomena cannot be explained by metapsychology, as Freud mistakenly believes. Metapsychology is itself dependent on the basis of clinical observation. However, Freud tries to justify his clinical interpretations by appealing to causal laws. To him, and also to Grünbaum, this appears to be the only way of validating interpretations. For the hermeneutician, as we argued earlier in connection with the "aliquis" example, such recourse to deductive-nomological explanation is only provisional and not a necessary condition for validity. He or she believes that the adequacy of interpretations may be assessed in different ways, as shown by historical work and demonstrated by discussions between psychotherapists on clinical matters. Usually, several interpretations are brought forward, some of which are rejected because they are at odds with accepted facts, others because of their inadequacy in respect to matters of transference, still others because they do not seem to fit into a coherent life history of the patiënt. A few interpretations stand up to criticism, possess a certain plausibility and pursuasiveness, and may be regarded as different angles from which we may enrich our understanding. The hermeneutical circle or ellipse is not a decision method to find out the truth, but it is a way of distinguishing between convincing knowledge and arbitrariness.

Here again, the fundamental difference between Grünbaum and the hermeneutic approach comes to light. For Grünbaum, the language of motivation and intention only makes sense when the possibility of reduction to an explanation through causes is granted (1984, p. 73). The hermeneutician will not challenge his right to apply the empirical-analytical method wherever he wishes. He will insist at the same time that actions may be understood in quite different ways by viewing them from emerging contexts. In such cases of hermeneutic understanding, there is no need to stay within the discourse of reasons and intentions and the relevance of causality dwindles into oblivion.

Grünbaum seems to reject this kind of interpretation without serious causal substantiation. He believes in the universal applicability of the empirical-analytical method and wishes to truncate the function of interpretation to a preliminary stage in research. In this respect we could say that he is defending an ontology, as it was described previously. One might ask if it would not clarify the possibilities and limits of the empirical-analytical approach to reality if it could be confronted with different approaches, as developed in hermeneutical philosophy.

It seems, however, that the empirical-analytical approach has been given a mythical status of absolute and exclusive validity. Speaking in metaphorical terms, the metaphor is absolutized and dead. The contrast between empirical-analytical and hermeneutic-interpretative knowledge is absolutized in a similar way: the two forms of knowledge are seen as opposites having nothing in common. Interpretations are disclaimed as knowledge because "they do not make a difference".

6. *A Hermeneutic Conception of Psychoanalysis*

The mere fact that Grünbaum misinterprets certain ideas in Habermas's early thought -- if it is granted that that is the case -- offers insufficient grounds to conclude that a hermeneutic conception of psychoanalysis is adequate. But it might be taken as evidence that it is very difficult, from an empirical-analytical point of view, to understand different approaches to reality. Their right of existence is denied from the outset. It is not our intention to present arguments for a hermeneutic approach to reality here. Carveth (1984) has given an interesting account of how this variation of hermeneutics might look in his presentation of a deconstructionist perspective on psychoanalysis. No doubt other hermeneutical approaches are possible, and it is one of the points of this article to argue that several perspectives may coexist and create a fruitful discussion, both in psychoanalytic theory and metatheory. Let us conclude by taking a closer look at some assumptions of present-day hermeneutics, and by making some comments on Habermas from a hermeneutical vantage point.

From the last century on, hermeneutics as the philosophical reflection on the art of interpretation, proceeds from the assumption that the relation between language and the world is problematic.[5] There is not one way of making pictures of facts (to use a phrase coined by Wittgenstein), but several ways, depending on different language games and, eventually, forms of life (Wittgenstein, 1953). This assumption -- stated negatively: language is not a universal grammatical model of representation -- is common to various schools of European thought such as hermeneutics (Gadamer), structuralism (De Saussure), and post-structuralism (Derrida, Lacan) as Frank (1984) has argued. It is also central in the work of the later Wittgenstein.

For psychoanalysis, adoption of these ideas implies that traditional metatheoretical notions of interpretation must be reevaluated. It is not to be expected, for example, that there is only one valid interpretation of a given action, dream, or biographical account. On the contrary, it is to be expected that several interpretations will be brought forward, none of which will turn out to be the best, though some interpretations may be regarded as defective or unconvincing.[6]

Ideally, an ongoing discussion between various alternative interpretations will be the result. On a practical level, clinical exchanges in psychoanalysis show that this is actually possible. Freud's case histories, for example, have been the subject of extensive discussions and reinterpretations by present-day analysts. New interpretations are a subject of discussion in the field and generally analysts do not seem to be worried that there are several alternatives to any given possibility (for the Case of Dora, see Bernheimer & Kahane 1985, Krohn & Krohn 1982).

On the metatheoretical level, however, things seem to be more complicated. Thinking philosophically, many analysts expect there *must* be methods to find out whether a given interpretation is correct or not. Thinking in that vein, Rosemary Sand (1983) has studied the Dora case history (Freud 1905) in order to find out how much evidence it provides for the theory of hysteria Freud was advancing around 1900. "The Dora case history could have served as an instance of corroboration of the theory if explanations offered therein had been based upon satisfactory evidence", she writes (Sand 1983, p. 356). As it turned out, this was not the case. In each instance but one, the evidence provided for the contentions under examination was unsatisfactory.

No doubt this conclusion also says something important about Freud as a theorist. But it might also mean that some expectations usually held by analysts need correction. Could it be that the lasting value of the case history lies in its creative use of "wild" interpretations, in the introduction of alternative ways of looking at neurotic symptoms, and in speculation on the theoretical level? In that case, Freud's reflection on his own work must be considered inadequate from the start. (This is not to deny the value of debates on particular interpretations given by Freud, with the aim of assessing their truth; see Sand 1983, Krohn & Krohn 1982).

An empirical-analytical approach would lead to the conclusion that psychoanalysis stands in dire need of scientific confirmation. Such a conclusion seems to leave us with only two options. Either one might reject psychoanalysis as a theory and a scientifically grounded form of therapy because one prefers not to work any longer on a theory with clinical foundations so weak and unpromising of further improvement (according to Grünbaum, 1984). Or one might try to find extraclinical evidence, reasoning that the problems of intraclinical testing are unsurmountable, whereas the credibility of psychoanalysis can only be improved by sound scientific research. Grünbaum reports that Eissler is thinking in this direction (p. 270).

However, there is still a third option open to us. We need not deny the legitimacy of the empirical-analytical approach inherent in the aforementioned options, but we may question its exclusivity. Thinking in the spirit of Sand (1983), we may reply to Grünbaum's criticisms of the weak evidential basis of psychoanalysis that we agree that this basis does not meet the requirements of empirical-analytic science, but that we are content with the kind of knowledge provided by psychoanalytical practice since Freud. We do not need laws, deductive-nomological explanations, and causal relationships; we feel confident restraining ourselves to the humble art of interpretation. Would that not be a viable alternative? It would at least enable us to answer simple questions like: How do analysts actually convince their colleagues when they don't provide confirmations for their theories? How do analysts get along in their daily work? What are all those debates in psychoanalysis about? The answer to the last question seems to be that analysts discuss the validity and adequacy of interpretations, not causal explanations. The quest for scientific status is strong though, like it is in academic psychology, where under the cover of empirical-analytical method more interpretative work is done than is usually acknowledged (Gergen 1985b). Conventional metatheory requires that psychologists, psychoanalysts, but also economists (McCloskey, 1983) claim they provide objective knowledge, c.q. deductive-nomological explanations.

This is the place to make some critical comments on Habermas' attempt to reconcile empirical-analytical method with hermeneutical understanding. In the opinion of the present author, Habermas accords too high a priority to the empirical-analytical approach. He makes a distinction between psychoanalysis and hermeneutic disciplines proper. Philology is concerned with the mutilated text of tradition; but it has to deal with accidental flaws only, according to Habermas: "For the meaning structure of the texts studied by hermeneutics is always threatened only by the impact of *external conditions*" (1978, p. 216). Whereas for psychoanalysis, "the omissions and distortions that it rectifies have a systematic role and function ... The mutilations have meaning *as such*". And so it: "*unites linguistic analysis with the psychological investigation of causal connections*" (Habermas 1978, p. 217).

First of all, the 'causal' connections that Habermas postulates are really pseudo-causal relations which are not used for prediction and control. The use of the word "causality" in this context may rightly be questioned. Don't these "pseudo-causal" relations form, like any other systematic distortion in texts, material for strict hermeneutical interpretation? Is speaking of causal and functional relations in regard to analytic theory not confusing and inappropriate, regarding the hermeneutic results of psychoanalysis? Bartels (1979) has argued for the latter with respect to Freud's dream interpretation. According to him, the dream story may be equated with other texts without further reservations. The dream, viewed as a series of situations, is incomprehensible because it cannot be integrated in our waking life. Bartels conceives this task of integration as a hermeneutic problem: a fusion of horizons must be achieved, the self-understanding of the individual has to be changed in the course of understanding the "absurdities" of the dream.

Secondly, Habermas stays close to Freud in emphasizing the unity of explanation and understanding. It is as if every act of the understanding of meaning must be legitimated by pointing to the causal connection which is uncovered in the same breath. But, though it is true in some cases that the meaning of a symptom or dream is connected to a specific repression, and though in these cases a causal connection between the repression and the meaning may be pointed out, this is by no means generally the case. The normal situation seems to be that any action or expression may, with the help of free association, be interpreted in multifarious ways in terms of several postulated repressions. This procedure is by no means futile, but it does not offer the "advantage" Habermas wished to retain, that is to say, that only one interpretation is correct and that we possess independent criteria to test its truth. It seems that the unity of explanation and understanding must be more radically questioned. There may be understanding without concomitant explanation; the reverse is probably not quite possible.

In the third place, the comment has to be made that very few hermeneutic philosophers would agree that understanding in general is disturbed by "accidental flaws only". There is a more fundamental difficulty inherent in every dialogue. Words do have relatively fixed meanings and may be repeated in that same meaning. But since we find ourselves engaged in an existing dialogue, it is impossible to anticipate what kind of understanding will be reached, transiently, for the time being.

A.A. Grünbaum, to return to him once more, was a more consistent supporter of the hermeneutic character of psychoanalysis. He regarded psychoanalysis as a hybrid discipline, with interpretative, but also scientistic elements. It is understandable, he argued, that acceptation of a new science within the framework of traditional scientific theorizing has a high priority. But psychoanalysis has a price to pay when it actually involves a new kind of knowledge. "Psychoanalysis will not be able to conquer its own position in the history of science by association with current assumptions and forms of thought, but only by stressing clearly an impulse to radical reevaluation of the concept of knowledge, present also in its simplest conceptions" (Grünbaum, 1928, p. 196). As we can see, in his rejection of scientism Grünbaum was far more radical than Habermas.

As a means of clarification, let us finally turn to the deconstructionist perspective as presented by Carveth (1984). Seen from this perspective (we might as well call it rhetorical or hermeneutical), psychoanalysis aims at transforming "dead" metaphors which shape the experience of a person on an unconscious level into "live" metaphors. Once an analysand learns that his unconscious fantasies shape his experience, and once he realizes that alternative metaphorical possibilities are open to him, he may overcome the determination of his life by metaphors that are a product of his early life history.

However, the analyst also uses metaphors. He has a set of theoretical concepts and notions of the analytic process which are largely borrowed from the work of Freud, and which in their turn result from unconscious fantasies and metaphors. These metaphors also have the tendency to lose their meaning. Ironically, this may be attributed to their incorporation in a theoretical system, where they develop a status of "truth" which makes them obsolete.

It could be argued, then, that developments in psychoanalysis are created by deconstructing dead metaphors central to classic psychoanalysis. Examples of such developments which may lead to an overthrow of dogmatism and dead metaphors are provided by discussions in regard to important interpretative schemata such as the Oedipal constellation (Edmunds, 1985) and at the psychohistorical research clarifying the roots of some of Freud's blind spots and dogmatic assertions (Swan, 1974; Krüll, 1985; Miller, 1984).

This interpretative work is matched by a growing sensibility to the methodology of interpretation. In the past decades, French & Fromm (1964), Cheshire (1975), Runyan (1982), and Bernstein (1983) have argued for a moderate hermeneutical position, with emphasis on methods for the evaluation of interpretations. From the hermeneutical point of view in the broad sense advocated here, it is perfectly possible to evaluate interpretations without expecting final answers or *the* truth. But is this a real disadvantage when we compare psychoanalysis to the situation in empirical-analytical psychology? Only to those who treat interpretations as degenerate untestable deductive-nomological explanations[7], does the hermeneutic approach in the humanities look like an intuitive and subjective affair.

Would this not form a more promising road towards epistemological respectability of psychoanalytic work than seemingly objective qualifications of psychoanalytic thought with predictable results such as formulated by Grunbaum (1984, p. 189) when he says that psychoanalysis is "alive, but - at least currently - hardly well, as it were" ?

7. *Conclusion*

The author agrees with Adolf Grünbaum that the scientific credentials of psychoanalysis are not impressive. Contrary to Grünbaum's opinion, this should be taken as evidence that psychoanalysis must not be interpreted as an empirical-analytical science. Grünbaum's arguments against one of the existing hermeneutical conceptions of psychoanalysis are shown to be unconvincing. Also, they indicate that for Grünbaum, empirical-analytical science incorporates the only sound approach to reality. It is argued that hermeneutics, in one or another of its various forms, provides an alternative approach leading to a different kind of knowledge. Viewing psychoanalysis along these lines means to situate it among the historical and cultural disciplines. The author believes this to be a more interesting and promising direction for the evaluation of psychoanalytic thought and especially for understanding its influences on contemporary society and academic discourse. In this conclusion, he finds himself in agreement with equally critical reactions towards Grünbaum's book by authors like Forrester (1986) and Sharpe (1986, 1988).

6

THE USE OF HERMENEUTICS IN PSYCHOLOGY: THE CASE OF ERGONOMICS

Contents:

1. *Introduction*

As I have argued elsewhere[1], we can look upon hermeneutics as one of the possible approaches to reality. The choice for an interpretative, or, alternatively, for an empirical-analytical approach, could be regarded as a pragmatical matter. A more radical approach claims that there are hermeneutical aspects in run-of-the-mill empirical-analytical research. Here I want to investigate the truth of this claim by looking at an example of what seems to be, on first sight, standard empirical-analytical research in ergonomics. The choice of the example is inspired by the feeling that it would be surprising for many of those involved that what is presented here is a form of interpretative psychology. I have chosen my case from the field of decision research, more precisely, from the ergonomic study of accidents. I will argue that even the most quantitative and analytical research has its interpretative aspects, because it is useless and uninteresting to quantify or analyse without knowing *how* and *what*. Therefore, in some way, be it implicitly or explicitly, quantitative research must be preceded by an interpretative stage. Sometimes research is entirely restricted to interpretation because there is no possibility or no need for predictions or hypothesis testing by prediction. On the other hand, there are also cases where the interpretative work is prepared in earlier work, and consequently research may be restricted to measurement of variables that are defined already. Normally we find a combination.

I will begin by defining the notion of hermeneutics, providing a list of characteristics. Then I will introduce the reader to some ways hermeneutics has been propagated as a method within psychology and discuss the views of D. Taylor (1987) in particular. Next comes the example of an ergonomic study which will be analyzed in detail. Finally, I will draw a few conclusions pertaining to existing meta-theory in psychology.

2. *Five characteristics of hermeneutics*

In chapter 1, I have situated the hermeneutic approach within philosophy of science. Hermeneutics may be conceived as a family of related approaches that are usually seen as a corrective to scientism. In the present context, the main thing is not to give an overview of the varieties within these approaches, but to provide the reader with a working definition, as it were, of hermeneutic studies. Based largely on the philosophical hermeneutics of H.G. Gadamer (1960), a number of presuppositions of interpretative investigations can be explicated. In the following list of five characteristics, I have drawn upon introductions into Gadamer's work, such as Widdershoven (1987), De Boer et al (1988), and Woolfolk et al (1988).

Interpretation according to hermeneutical philosophy may be defined as the search for meaning, truth, and knowledge without being committed to scientific method as used by empirical-analytical science. The claim of hermeneutics is that truth may be found outside the realm of science. Interpretation is concerned with anything possessing human significance, such as texts, actions, historical events, human artefacts, art, facial and bodily expressions, music, and the development of technology. It is characterized by the following features.

a. *The hermeneutical circle.* The interpreter views phenomena as parts dependent on larger structures. One relies on a preconception about the whole in understanding the parts. The understanding of the parts is fed into the global preconception. This has been described as a cyclical procedure and it is regarded as impossible to start somewhere on a firm basis. Indeed, there is an unavoidable circularity in this non-empiricist epistemological view, though it is regarded as non-vicuous (cf. Woolfolk et al 1988, p. 7).

b. *Internal relations.* Interpretation is directed to the meaningful (internal) relations between actions and events, not to their statistical or lawful (external) relations. An example of an internal relation is that between an action and a motive. Though we may observe that the two go together regularly, we only speak of a "good motive" if we are able to understand the action as springing from the motive - of course presupposing a cultural background.

c. *Individual cases.* Since hermeneutics does not aim to find laws, interpretation may be, but does not have to be, directed at individual cases. This is not to say that no general insights may be assembled. However, the first ambition of hermeneutics is to understand individual cases, apart from the question whether the insights could apply to other cases as well. There is no need to aim at prediction; understanding is possible without knowledge of laws (or external relations).

d. *Fusion of horizons.* Both the interpreter and those interpreted have a conception of the world and truth. The author of a text, for instance, also has a claim to truth. Interpretation may be seen as a dialogue between interpreter and text, between 'subject' and 'object', with the aim of removing obstacles for understanding. The ideal end result would be that both sides share the same perspective of the matter concerned. That would mean a fusion of the different horizons of understanding.

e. *Application.* Interpretation is part of history. This means, first, that the interpreter stands in the same tradition as his interpretandum; usually there is a shared cultural heritage. Second, interpretation is an application of insights from the past to the present situation. Even an insight in remotest history needs to be put in the context of actuality, and, indeed, has arisen from preconceptions formed in the present context. This also implies that there is a rhetorical context in which interpretation takes place. There is an audience which has to be persuaded of the truth claimed by the interpretation.

3. *Psychologists on Hermeneutics*

Within the present framework, it is impossible to provide an oversight of hermeneutical approaches in psychology. The ideas on hermeneutics and dominant methodology in psychology, to be discussed in this section, will only be presented briefly in so far as they possess immediate relevance for our problem.

Martin Packer (1985) has argued for a hermeneutical approach of human conduct in a Heideggerian fashion. Packer draws upon Heidegger's notion of the ready-to-hand mode (*Zuhandenheit*) to indicate the object of research for hermeneutical psychology. "What the hermeneutic investigator studies, then, is what people actually do when they are engaged in the everyday practical tasks of life rather than in the detached contemplation that characterizes pencil-and-paper tasks and most interview situations. Interviewing tells us primarily about the present-at-hand [i.e. theoretical; *Vorhandenheit*] mode" (1985, p. 1086). In other words, hermeneutics aims at understanding human action in its natural context, whereas dominant methodologies in psychology tend to reduce action to its more abstract elements. "This dependence of the 'facts' of human phenomena on their setting is covered up by the empiricist and rationalist approaches, both of which attempt to study objective elements of human action and social relations, refusing to acknowledge their historically situated character" (ibid).

In regard to the type of explanation provided by hermeneutics, Packer maintains that it doesn't look for formal structures or causal laws, but seeks to elucidate and make explicit our practical everyday understanding of human actions. "It is a historically situated approach, regarding explanation as first and foremost the giving of an account that is sensible in the way it addresses current interests and concerns, not a search for timeless and ahistorical laws and formal structures" (1985, p. 1088). Packer warns his audience that the product of hermeneutical inquiry does not seem to meet the standards of scientific rigor that psychologists have usually been taught. The end product is more modest in its aims than a causal law or a formal model. Yet it is "subtle and complex, intellectually satisfying, and more appropriate to human action, embracing the historical openness, the ambiguity and opacity .... that action manifests" (1985, p. 1092).

From a different perspective, that of Gadamer's hermeneutics, Susan Hekman (1984) has proposed ideas that can be seen as complementary to Packer's. Her concern is to overcome the dichotomy between the positivist and the humanist approaches to social action. Positivists attempt to replace the actors' subjective concepts with the 'objective' concepts of the social scientist. Humanists attempt to describe meaningful action strictly in the social actors' terms. Hekman interprets Gadamer as an alternative to both extremes: according to him, understanding a text involves the fusion of the conceptual schemes, or horizons, of author and interpreter. In the case of actions, the horizons of actors and scientists are involved: the scientist may impose his conceptual scheme as long as he does not deny the constitutive role of the social actors' concepts. Thus a dialogue, or a form of research that resembles a dialogue, is needed.

What I want to emphasize here is the common thread in Packer and Hekman: the investigator should not forget that she is dealing with a subject matter that has a structure of its own. Action is structured by specific language games and psychologists cannot get around that fact: it is necessary to study the language games. Another thing Packer and Hekman have in common is their rejection of the subjectivist alternative: that would mean giving up the core of the scientific enterprise altogether.

These few remarks do not render justice to the intricacies of Hekman's and Packer's arguments, nor to the theoretical backdrop of a hermeneutical approach. They are only meant to bring some fairly obvious points into the limelight, things almost too trivial to mention, but with more than trivial consequences for research. In a previously mentioned essay on the so-called 'Methodological Imperative' in psychology, Kurt Danziger (1985a) creates a similar impression by demanding the attention of his readership for observations about empirical psychology which are well-known. The curious thing is that nobody ever asks for the rationale of certain methodological habits in psychology, even though they seem to be strangely irrational and unmotivated on closer inspection. Here I will only mention Danziger's main point: in empirical psychology, methodological considerations are given priority over substantive psychological considerations. The requirements of the dominant empiricist methodology are constitutive for the facts (observations, evidence) that are taken as the subject matter and for the theories that are constructed on the basis of them. A *methodological* circle is the result: methods based on assumptions about the nature of the subject matter only produce observations which must confirm these assumptions. The largely implicit agreement on methodology among academic psychologists is seen by Danziger as the main constituent of the present-day psychological paradigm. In the domination of institutionalized methodology over psychology, three commonly-held beliefs seem to be ripe for revision, according to Danziger. "(1) That statistical inference provides the only valid procedure for relating data and theory; (2) that the rules about what constitutes valid evidence are independent of theory and are valid forever; (3) that the structure of theory must be accommodated to the structure of methodology and not vice versa" (1985a, p. 13).

Danziger's aim is to analyze dominant empirical-analytical psychology, to show its presuppositions and their consequences. Though he doesn't even mention the hermeneutical approach as an alternative, it is striking that he is in basic agreement with the hermeneutical analyses sketched earlier. In short: the subject matter of psychology has a structure of its own. Psychologists cannot hide behind their methodological commitments, they have to go out into the world and study this structure which comes in a multitude of forms, languages, and customs.

What the theoreticians, mentioned so far, seem to agree on might be put like this: the hermeneutical approach does not form a methodology radically different from the empirical-analytical approach. It is better to consider it as a mode of reflection on research in psychology which has implications for any work done in the field. Thinking along these lines, we may abandon the idea of two possible approaches existing alongside within psychology, one consistently empiricist, the other purely hermeneutical. With this tentative idea in mind, I would like to take a look at the ideas of Donald Taylor, who has proposed hermeneutics as an approach within ergonomics.

In a stimulating paper, Taylor (1987) suggests that the doctrine of mechanism is in decline in the field of ergonomics (viewed as the study of man-machine systems). Ergonomics, like all behavioral sciences, has traditionally relied on a mechanistic, deterministic, ultimately predictable model of man. In recent times, however, it is becoming apparent that there are basic weaknesses in this doctrine. In the study of safety and accidents, the scientist is confronted with the freedom of his subject matter: "it can seem almost as if the public is out to defeat safety measures by finding new ways of having accidents in an increasingly safer world" (Taylor 1987, p. 32). For this and other reasons, Taylor proceeds from the assumption that, regarding accidents, the limit of mechanistic explanation has been reached. Hermeneutics is offered as an alternative approach. The explanations sought by hermeneuticians are not "likely to be generally true, nor quantitatively expressed" (p. 33). Since the terms used in hermeneutical enquiry are "reasons, meanings, intentions, actions, desires, etc...., words used in common discourse" (p. 34), it would be a mistake to add them to a scientific discourse. That would be to mix two levels of explanation, Taylor warns.

As it turns out, with the hermeneutic vocabulary proposed by Taylor, it is very difficult, if not impossible, to explain accidents. "The meaning of an action which happens to lead to an accident cannot include any reference to the accident, because then to intend the action would be to intend the accident: a contradiction in terms .... It is proposed as an hypothesis that accidents uniquely comprise an anomaly of meaning: a kind of 'black hole' in the universe of meaning, which cannot be explained in the same terms as the rest of the space. Accidents may thus be regarded as truly *meaningless events*" (Taylor 1987, p. 35). Even though accidents are not intended, one might try to ascribe some meaning to them in a broader context. Does this make sense? "Looking for causes is one such activity, both in the particular case and in general. Many papers in accident literature refer to the *causes* of accidents, as if this would explain why they happened, by linking them to meaningful antecedents in the framework of inductive generalization, i.e., to predict that other accidents would happen in similar circumstances.... For example, to say that an accident was caused by faulty brakes is to say that vehicles with brakes in that condition are liable to accident, that the accident would not have occurred if the brakes had not been faulty, etc.; but it is not to explain actions leading to the existence of the faulty brakes as being careless, unskilled, motivated by false economy, etc. The latter type of meaning ascription is often used in allocating blame: another kind of explanation of the accident" (p. 36).

These views about the meaninglessness of accidents are questionable. There are two of Taylor's assumptions I would like to take issue with. First, if he speaks about the meaninglessness of accidents, what Taylor really wants to say is that accidents are meaningless to the actors involved. Those involved tend to think that accidents are 'impossible' and deny meaning to the accident because they fail to see the relevant connections between their own antecedent actions and the accident. However, from a research perspective, we shouldn't be afraid to ascribe meaning to the accident by investigating the context. As Taylor himself says, "we seek to understand events in the world by reference to their meaning, not usually in isolation, but with reference to the whole cultural environment in which they occur" (p. 36). This is exactly what we have to do with accidents. Being investigators, psychologists should simply not accept their apparent meaninglessness. Why does Taylor think so? This brings me to a second and more basic assumption he makes.

Taylor's understanding of hermeneutics is that it accepts the point of view of the actors, their structuring of the world, without any critical questioning. As he puts it, "the meanings of actions have to be interpreted in the light of the agents' motives, purposes, principles and beliefs, indeed from the whole social context in which the actions take place" (p. 37). Now, if we accept the truth of the first part of this quotation, accidents are obviously meaningless because they are unintended. But as we have seen earlier in this section, hermeneuticians from various origins do not accept this at all (see Hekman's rejection of humanism). They assume, much more sensibly as I would argue, that actions have to be interpreted in the whole context in which the action takes place (see the latter part of the last quotation), and this context comprises much more than the actors' intentions.

Adoption of this modern notion of hermeneutics as a virtual dialogue between investigators and subjects of research, aiming at a fusion of horizons, solves some of the difficulties and paradoxes created by Taylor. We no longer have to be puzzled by the meaninglessness of accidents -- we appreciate that this depends on the perspective taken. This encourages a broader analysis of accidents than asking for the agents' intentions alone. Also, this enables us to look into the possibility of other preventive measures than those suggested by Taylor. As a working hypothesis, he maintains rather dogmatically that the man-machine interface cannot be further improved (p. 33), and that the promulgation of safety is a matter of social influence (p. 39). But why should a hermeneutical investigation not lead to an improvement of the working environment? In the next section we will see an example of this. In any case the possibility cannot and should not be ruled out by theoretical considerations.

In conclusion, I have argued that Taylor has introduced an unnecessary and unfruitful dichotomy between the doctrines of mechanism and hermeneutics. The next section is meant to demonstrate that a combination of hermeneutical assumptions and causal analysis is actually possible.

4. *Analysis of an Example*

The example I have chosen is an investigation into the causation and possible prevention of accidents at sea (Wagenaar & Groeneweg 1987). Let me first comment on this choice: in what respects is it a typical example of empirical-analytical research in psychology? The best answer I can give to this question is: I don't know; I'm afraid it is not typical at all, but my analysis, as I hope, may still illuminate the use of hermeneutics in psychological research. The example, as will be seen, is empirical-analytical in its outlook for various reasons:

a. It is an attempt to analyze accidents and their context into causative factors;

b. The results are presented in a quantitative form;

c. The research is performed in the field of ergonomics, usually regarded as a 'hard' science, where most researchers believe that mechanistic models of man are appropriate (cf. D. Taylor 1987; Taylor's proposal is an exceptional case).

d. 'Accidents at sea' is a highly technical subject, creating the impression that it may adequately be approached in the empirical-analytical way.

The investigation of Wagenaar & Groeneweg has practical aims [how are accidents best prevented?] but also theoretical pretentions. It is not an example of abstract theorizing, nor is it simply practical.

The assumptions of Wagenaar & Groeneweg are the following. "Accidents in complex man-machine systems are usually caused by a multitude of events which occur in a coincidental manner that was never foreseen ... It is the thesis of this study that among these causes human error is the category which is most simply controlled. However, such a control can be exerted only by change of the work environment ..." (1987, p. 587). The fruitfulness of these assumptions is tested by an analysis of 100 accidents at sea. In each accident, the chain of causes leading to the accident is reconstructed and the nature of the causes is assessed. Subsequently, the human errors among these causes are classified. "The nature of these errors will give some insight into the underlying processes and, hopefully, provide a clue as how to prevent errors" (p. 588).

The method of causal analysis used by Wagenaar & Groeneweg deserves special attention. The raw material used in their study consists of reports by the Dutch Shipping Council, the national authority responsible for the legal investigation of accidents at sea. The accident scenarios provided by the Council are translated into logical trees, consisting of events, connected by logical AND-gates and OR-gates. An example is the following diagram (to be read from left to right):

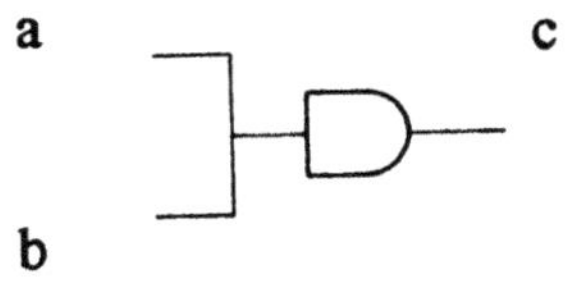

(If only causes a and b are both present, they lead to result c.) So, a and b are necessary conditions, and D is an AND-gate. Another example of combining causes looks like this:

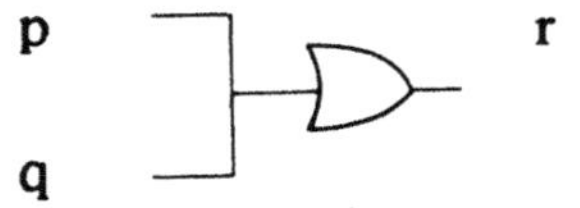

where p *or* q is sufficient to cause r. So, p and and q are sufficient conditions and the symbol  stands for an OR-gate.

The results of applying this method of causal analysis to a sample of 100 accidents at sea can be summarized as follows. The total number of causes was 2250, out of which 345 were forms of human error. The human errors were all necessary conditions and therefore crucial; only four of the 100 accidents occurred without any preceding human error. Since the essential task of man in complex systems consists of preventing or counteracting the errors, the contribution of human error to the accidents cannot be considered marginal, as Wagenaar & Groeneweg argue (p. 594). Insight into the nature and coincidence of error may be obtained from tables 3 and 4, taken from Wagenaar & Groeneweg (1987, p. 594-5).

Table 3
Number of human errors and erring persons in 100 accidents at sea

No. of people involved	Number of human errors 0	1	2	3	4	5	6	7	8	9	10	Total
0	4	-	-	-	-	-	-	-	-	-	-	4
1	-	3	18	14	6	4	-	-	-	-	-	45
2	-	-	4	11	16	7	2	1	-	-	-	41
3	-	-	-	1	-	3	2	1	1	-	-	8
4	-	-	-	-	-	-	1	-	-	-	1	2
Total	4	3	22	26	22	14	5	2	1	0	1	100

Table 4
Classification of human errors in 100 accidents at sea, according to Feggetter's classification system

No.	Feggetter's category	Overall frequency of errors	Number of accidents in which the errors occur
	Cognitive system		
1.1	Human information processing	44	35
1.2	Visual illusions	2	2
1.3	False hypothesis	60	51
1.4	Habits	50	46
1.5	Motivation	1	1
1.6	Training	41	35
1.7	Personality	43	35
1.8	Fear	0	0
Subtotal (%)		70%	93%
	Social system		
2.1	Social pressure	20	17
2.2	Role	2	2
2.3	Life stress	2	2
Subtotal (%)		7%	21%
	Situational system		
3.1	Physical stress	18	12
3.2	Environmental stress	22	17
3.3	Ergonomic aspects	39	34
Subtotal (%)		23%	56%

These data lead the researchers to reject the explanation that accidents result from conscious risk-taking. As they argue: "Accidents appear to be the result of highly complex coincidences which could rarely be foreseen by the people involved. The unpredictability is caused by the large numer of causes and by the spread of information over participants. Also the nature of the errors that are made indicates lack of understanding rather than lack of motivation or risk propensity. Accidents occur because the behaviour that causes them is not seen as risky. Errors of information processing (mostly lack of attention) are made frequently, but are, under normal conditions, not punished by accidents. Hypotheses that proved to be false in the reported incidents were usually correct in previous instances, and that is exactly the reason why they are adopted again, even when the contrary information is available (cf. Reason, 1986). Habits that contribute to the origin of accidents could become habits because they were not negatively rewarded before. The same can be said about lack of training and unsuitable personality. These factors, lack of attention, false hypotheses, wrong habits, lack of training and adverse personality were at the bottom of 93 out of 100 accidents. Each of these factors interferes with risk evaluation because people have no insight in the complex conjunctions of which the factors form the necessary ingredients ... It follows from the foregoing that accidents cannot be prevented just by telling people to act safely. The behaviours leading to accidents are not considered unsafe at the time. If these behaviours are to be prevented nonetheless, we should be prepared to change the environment by which they are elicited" (Wagenaar & Groeneweg 1987, p. 596-7). And so the conclusion is that the acts which (very rarely) lead to an accident are part of a causal network so complex, that it cannot be overseen by the actors. Human errors are not recognized as errors and, consequently, though they are at the basis of almost every accident, they cannot be avoided by motivating or instructing people. This sounds like a strangely unhermeneutical conclusion. It appears that human motives and cognitions cannot be influenced and that Wagenaar & Groeneweg, in Taylor's words, operate under the 'doctrine of mechanism' (see above, section 3). In what sense could the study presented here be called hermeneutical? Let us turn to the five characteristics presented in section 2 to get a precise answer to this question.

a. *The hermeneutic circle.* As we have seen, hermeneuticians maintain that understanding inevitably involves reference to that which is already known. The hermeneutic circle describes the contextual nature of knowledge: the object of study is seen as a part depending for its meaning on the whole structure it belongs to. This structure may be a language game, a form of life, a set of rules, a text, or a legal system.

In order to see whether such a circle is operative in the research under scrutiny, we can look at one example of an accident described in detail by Wagenaar & Groeneweg. It concerns an 'impossible' accident on the Ms. Farmsum.

"On 14 December 1982 on board the Farmsum sailing on the Atlantic Ocean, four men were busy cleaning hold 6. Suddenly the 15 meter high and 25 meter wide partition between hold 5 and 6 collapsed and 6000 tons of water flooded over the unsuspecting men. Three sailors were thrown up against a metal wall by the torrent and drowned. The bosun was miraculously saved. It is absolutely certain that all the men assumed that hold 5 was empty. In everyone's opinion the accident was impossible. An analysis of the investigation following the accident revealed a complex chain of causes leading to the accident.

Cleaners were working in hold 6 while hold 5 was full of water. No one was aware of this fact, and the wall between hold 5 and 6 was not designed to withstand this pressure. The situation is represented as shown in Fig. 1.

How could hold 5 be full of water without anyone being aware of it? The ship sailed with water in hold 4 as ballast. Due to bad weather, a leak had sprung between hold 4 and 5. Thus hold 5 filled up with water from hold 4. It had been noticed that water was disappearing from hold 4, but the first mate had a very plausible explanation for this. While cleaning hold 6, sluice water had been used. However, it appeared to be impossible to pump this water out because the sluice valve in hold 4 had been left open by mistake. This caused the sluice pump not to pump from hold 6 but from hold 4. The first mate responded to this by refilling hold 4. Thus, more than 24 hours before the accident we see the chain of causes shown in Fig. 2" (Wagenaar & Groeneweg 1987, p. 590-1).

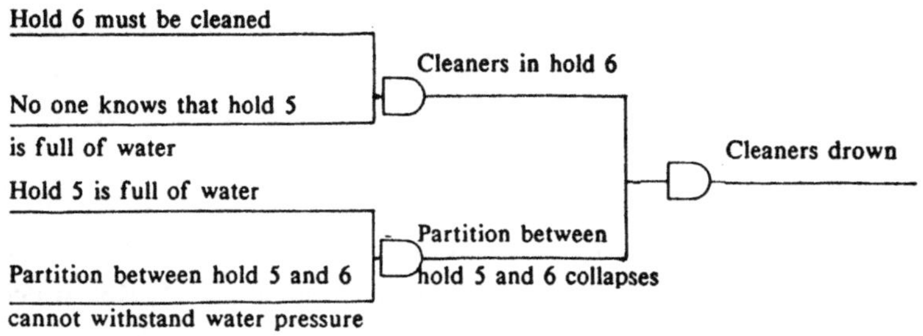

Fig. 1. Causes leading to the drowning of cleaners in hold 6

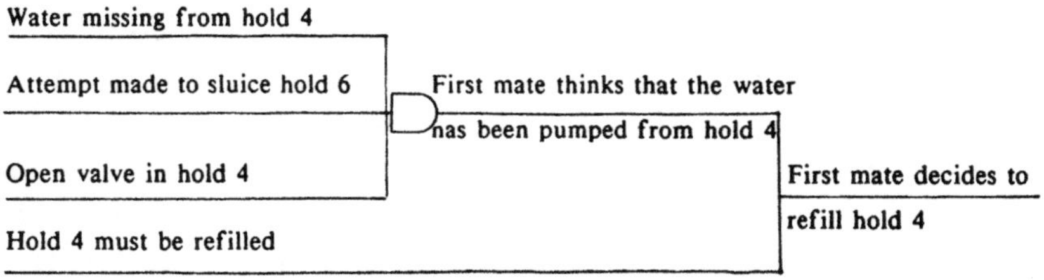

Fig. 2. Chain of causes leading to the first mate refilling hold 4.

(Figures from Wagenaar & Groeneweg, p. 591)

Before proceeding with the analysis, it must be noted that the investigation of the accident is based on a familiarity with the technical and organizational aspects of working on ships. These global preconceptions are tested against the facts: the details of the events in this case. This may lead to a revision of the preconceptions, etc., etc. Neither the investigation of the Shipping Council, nor the causal analysis based on the facts of the investigation would have made sense without such a thorough prescientific understanding.

b. *Internal Relations.* Instead of securing nomological relations between logically unrelated variables, hermeneutics is interested in meaning relations or internally related variables. A causal analysis, as applied to the accidents, has the appearance of assessing empirical relations between events. These events, however, and especially the actions among them, are meaningfully related. Look for instance at Figure 2. The two events: "First mate thinks that the water has been pumped from hold 4" and "First mate decides to refill hold 4" are not only causally, but also meaningfully related. There are motivations and beliefs involved.

This is also clear when we listen to the reasoning of the investigators which backs this particular causal tree. "It seems rather absurd that the first mate thought the large amount of water missing from hold 4 could have been pumped out by a low capacity sluice pump. However, we must realize that the first mate did not know how long the pumping had been going on, or how much water had been removed. At that point this was not so important because the officer was busy trying to solve a very different problem. He tried to explain why the water could not be pumped from hold 6. Initially he thought that the sluice pump was broken. The men in the machine room knew for certain that this pump had worked. The discovery of the open valve in hold 4 offered a new hypothesis, and the missing water confirmed this hypothesis. It is known that people accept hypotheses on the grounds of confirming information, without critically testing the hypotheses (Lord, Lepper & Ross, 1979). The first mate was satisfied with the confirmation, shut off the sluice valve and started to fill hold 4.

Approximately 3300 tons of water were missing from hold 4. The first mate did not notice that this had been replenished by a total of 6600 tons, almost more than hold 4 could accommodate. Naturally the explanation was that hold 4 as well as hold 5 were filled. The fact that the first mate was not present during the original filling of hold 4 takes its revenge here. He could not know that this had only lasted a few hours and he did not make a rough calculation on the grounds of pump capacity. He did not order someone to keep an eye on the refilling of hold 4. This chain of events is represented in Fig. 3"

(Wagenaar & Groeneweg, p. 591-2).

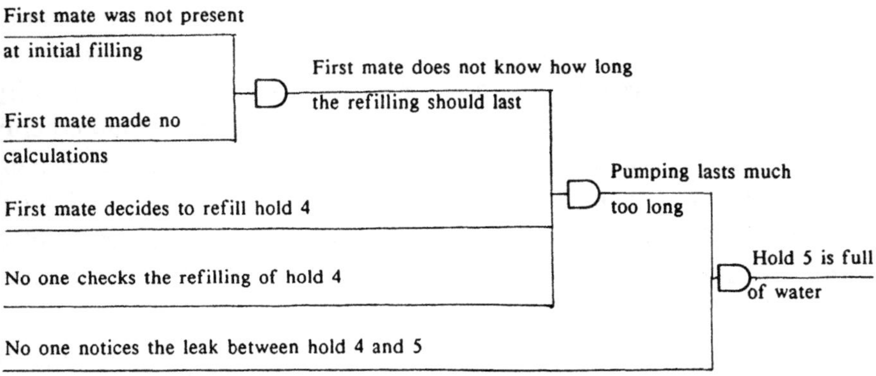

Fig. 3. Chain of events leading to hold 5 being full of water

The causal analysis, as it appears, depends on an understanding of the logic of the situation: the motives and beliefs of the actors are taken into consideration. Only on the basis of such an understanding can certain decisions and actions be credited with causal relevance in a particular causal tree. Causal analysis thus means: rational reconstruction.

c. *Individual cases.* The aim of hermeneutical investigation has been indicated as an understanding of particular events, rather than a search for generalizations and laws of nature. Since Wagenaar & Groeneweg reach general conclusions, and since they claim to provide advice relevant to the prevention of accidents in general, their aims seem to be in conflict with hermeneutics. Nevertheless, I suggest this conclusion rests on a misunderstanding. There is nothing contradictory in the notion of quantifying hermeneutical results. A fundamental problem would arise first, and then an attempt at understanding emerges.

Let me try to elucidate this by approaching the problem from a different angle. Danziger (1985a) has drawn attention to a strong belief among psychologists that aggregate data from many individuals form the only acceptable basis for making general theoretical claims about individuals. This has led to the widespread use of samples of individuals in experimentation. "In principle, there is no reason why one should restrict oneself to sampling individuals; one could equally well sample situations or the actions of a single individual. However, there have only been rare instances of this in the psychological literature ..." as Danziger (1985, p. 6) comments. (An example of a sample of actions from one individual is given by Wagenaar (1986a) in his study of his own memory.)

Now it seems to me that this psychological practice, regarded by Danziger as a consequence of what he calls the "methodological imperative", is a clear example of how empirical-analytical research tends to exclude individual cases. It does so without real necessity, by quantifying at the wrong moment. If one puts individuals together in groups before even having looked at their individual behavior, it is clear that one will never learn anything about individual behavior; the results are about group averages, and will be restricted to group averages, or the non-existing "average individual".

Another approach is to study individual cases first, and put the data concerning individuals together in a later phase. In that case, which is the case of the causal analysis of accidents, we have a hermeneutical study with a subsequent statistical-quantitative elaboration of the data gathered about individuals. In other words, not all quantitative research is empirical-analytical, and not all hermeneutical studies are "qualitative": the opposition between qualitative and quantitative research, or Clinical versus Scientific Methods, is an ill-conceived dichotomy, as is sometimes admitted by those who use the concepts (cf. Berg & Smith 1985, p. 15).

d. *Fusion of Horizons.* The subject and the object of study co-participate in a fusion of horizons in which the understanding of the interpreter and the self-understanding of those whose life (words, actions) is interpreted are involved in a game of mutual influence. The aim is a reconciliation of the different perspectives, or at least an understanding of the discrepancies.

As will be clear by now, the perspectives of the actors involved do play a part in the causal analysis of Wagenaar & Groeneweg, even though they are sometimes seen as faulty or limited, or based on erroneous observations or false conclusions. A few examples: "It seems rather absurd that the first mate thought ... we must realize that [he] did not know ... he tried to explain why ... initially he thought that ... he could not know ..." (p. 591-2). The crux of the problem was that each of the (at least five) actors in the drama had his own perspective: each of them could only oversee one part of the scenario. The investigators are able to oversee the whole situation, though only with the benefit of hindsight. There is no need to scorn the actors for their ignorance, at least not in every case; the investigators may learn a great deal from considering the exact perspective open to an actor involved in a certain situation.

The method of causal analysis adopted by Wagenaar & Groeneweg is thus a sensitive instrument of investigation. The investigator must reconstruct the beliefs and motives of the actors, and become familiar with the rules in force in a particular situation. This puts him in the position of an interpreter who brings his own presuppositions into play, rather than in the position of a scientist merely testing hypotheses. The interpreter is able to improve his knowledge of the situation by listening to his objects of investigation who act from their own perspectives. He need not regard his own view of the situation as superior, even though the overview provided by the investigation may enable him to get a comprehensive view in the end. The scientist lacks this dimension of research.

In psychology there have been some interesting discussions in the past between theoreticians who regarded their own solutions as far more rational than their experimental subjects, and others who denounced the habit of viewing ordinary people as mere "scientists manqué". (See the criticism directed at Nisbett & Ross by White, 1980).

As a final note regarding the fusion of horizons, it could be said that Wagenaar & Groeneweg, in their causal analysis, approach the accidents and the actors involved from the postulates of the dialogue, and not from the postulates of empirical-analytical science, using terms from De Boer (1983a). The postulates of empirical-analytical science -- analyzability and lawfulness of the object (see chapters 1 and 4 in this book) would exclude considerations about the rationality or irrationality of the actors involved, because they imply a view of man as a determined generalized machine. One is reminded here of Taylor's 'doctrine of mechanism'. The postulates of the dialogue, on the other hand, enable us to deal with people as free and responsible beings (characteristics which may not be obvious at any moment). They are close to the attitude we have to our fellow beings in daily life: we expect them to be intentional, truthful, rational, unique, and authentic (De Boer 1983a, chapter 8; see also 1985a).

It must be admitted that Wagenaar & Groeneweg, in the conclusions they draw from their study, are not optimistic about improving the rationality (or motivation) of people as a remedy for preventing accidents. But that only means they defend a certain view on human rationality; they do not adopt a mechanistic doctrine, neither in the methods they proclaim for controlling human behavior, nor in the way they conduct the research.

Also, it must be realized that the method of causal analysis, as used in the present context, is dependent on a previous investigation of accidents by experts of the Shipping Council. This means that many important decisions - for instance, concerning the categorization of events - have been made even before the scientific analysis started. Also, the setting of a time horizon in the causal analysis - how far back in history the analysis should go - was decided by following limits adopted by the Council (p. 589). This means that an important phase in conducting the research is not reflected in the account of this study: the confrontation with reality as not yet interpreted from without. That particular phase probably contains particularly hermeneutical aspects in any study.

e. *Application.* Hermeneuticians claim that the interpreter is part of history and any interpretation of past events includes an application of the insights to the present situation. The effects a given interpretation might have on the people involved are part of this problem. Do we find any reflection of this problem in the study of Wagenaar & Groeneweg? The practical nature of their conclusions makes considerations of these matters urgent. Any measure proposed to reduce the risk of accidents has various complicated effects on behavior which may turn out to outweigh the risk-reducing effects partially or completely (see Wagenaar, 1987a, for an example).

Indeed, the practical changes advocated by Wagenaar are motivated by a consideration of human possibilities. As he argues, in reaction to a critical notice by Hofstee (1987), we cannot sensibly inform people about certain small risks, or warn them of the harmful consequences of these risks, when people believe there is no possibility of an accident, and do not view their behavior in terms of risk taking (Wagenaar 1987c). As the study on accidents at sea says, "errors do not look like errors at the same time they are perpetrated, and the accidents that are caused by them look impossible beforehand ... telling people to change their behaviour when facing accidents will not help, because they will rarely believe they are facing accidents" (Wagenaar & Groeneweg 1987, p. 598). In other words, simply telling people in highly complicated environments how things really work is useless when we do not take their cognitive capacities into consideration. For that reason, a better solution may be found in improving the man-machine interface, to change the environment. More precisely, "It is possible to secure the attention of operators, for instance by providing them with continuous tasks and knowledge of results. The number of false hypotheses can be reduced by the introduction of intelligent support systems, like the IMAS system proposed by Embrey & Humphreys (1984). Undesirable habits can be largely eliminated, not by instruction or indoctrination (cf. Slovic, 1985) but by control and incentives. Training can be improved and maintained. The effect of adverse personality and social pressure can be reduced through the creation of better working conditions" (Wagenaar & Groeneweg 1987, p. 597-8). Having reached the end of this long exposition, let us turn to an evaluation of a few specific problems in regard to the connection between hermeneutics and empirical-analytical research.

5. *Evaluation*

My conclusion will come as no big surprise to the reader: there is nothing contradictory in a combination of hermeneutical and empirical-analytical research. Moreover, the two should be combined as much as possible in every suitable case. We should regard 'pure' empirical-analytical research with suspicion: there is always an implicit hermeneutical and rhetorical dimension in studies in the humanities. Research begins and ends with interpretations (made consciously or automatically, as a habit) of both the phenomena studied and the theory used to describe, explain, or manipulate them.

We might order the variety of studies done in psychology on a scale running from highly predictable, repeatable phenomena to the other extreme of highly individual, unique, and unpredictable events. In a decision situation which stays structurally the same, we may develop expert systems and models which, in the end, facilitate optimal decisions in every instance. There are other situations in human life that have to be structured continuously. Psychotherapists are faced with such problems - and of course they find ways to reduce them to relevant variables they feel able to handle. But also in decision theory there is a growing awareness that many problems have to be structured before they can be handled in a quantitative ("scientific") way (see Westenberg 1988, Vlek 1987). D. Taylor points to the fact that evaluation research "is an active and growing field, which is both localized in its application and developmental in nature" (1987, p. 40).

So we see a shift in interest in psychology from grand theories and universal generalizations towards local models and providing information for decision-makers about programs of intervention. I interpret this development as a growing sensibility for the necessity of a hermeneutical approach. On the one hand, the object of psychology - human action - is studied seriously in its natural context. That is to say, not via the detour of animal behavior or artificial experimental settings, but in the concrete appearance of the language games of real life. On the other hand, one has become aware that it doesn't make sense to study 'behavior' without knowing what it means: it is not a methodological question what the 'facts' are, but a theoretical-psychological matter. There seems to be a liberation from Danziger's methodological imperative.

"But what is the difference between the hermeneutical approach and empirical research which is conducted thoughtfully according to methodological rules written down by me already in 1961?" I was asked this question by Dutch psychologist Prof. A.D. de Groot, author of the well-known book *Methodology*[2]. Let me conclude by answering it. I can be brief, because my answer is implied by the foregoing. It makes no sense to create a dichotomy between two methodological approaches. What I have called empirical-analytical research is relevant and interesting only if the analysis is performed judiciously. And this means that something is required which I have referred to as hermeneutics, but it may as well be called 'thinking backward' (Einhorn & Hogarth 1987, Wagenaar 1987b) or 'creativity', 'intuition', or whatever you like. The simple thing is, we can never start counting and measuring or use strict rules of inference before we have spent some real thought about the matter under scrutiny. Many psychologists are not aware of this aspect of their research (sometimes they suffer under the old-fashioned prejudice that it is not allowed to use your intuition or creativity) but they still do interesting research. In this case it is a matter of changing the metatheory (cf. McCloskey (1983) on the 'Rhetoric of Economics'). Other psychologists are so much inhibited by the methodological imperative and the neglect of the hermeneutical dimension that the quality of their work is affected. I think this is what Roe (1989) is worried about when he speaks about psychology's 'free-floating knowledge', asking with what kind of people all those empirical studies deal[3]. Indeed, this is a more serious problem. I have tried to make some suggestions in this chapter what to do about it.

7

A RHETORICAL APPROACH TO DREAM THEORIES AND DREAMS

> At once it struck me, what quality went to form a Man of Achievement .... - I mean *Negative Capability*, that is when man is capable of being in uncertainties, Mysteries, doubts, without any irritable reaching after fact & reason -
>
> John Keats.

Contents

1. *The Rhetorical Approach in Psychology*

In recent years, there has been a growing interest in what is called the 'rhetoric of inquiry'. Those who think along rhetorical lines question the absolutized dichotomy between truth and opinion they view in traditional approaches to the humanities and especially the social sciences. Rhetoricians maintain that persuasion is needed in defending any truth; we can merely aim for the plausible and the probable. Tempting visions of absolute certitudes are to be rejected in favor of modest attempts to understand the subtleties of actual argument in various disciplines.

The development of this field so far has been sketched by Nelson

& Megill (1986, 1987). They indicate some important threads in rhetorical thought in philosophy and the humanities. First, there is the philosophical attack on foundationalism. As indicated in chapter 1, there is a growing doubt that it will ever be possible to formulate absolute standards of criticism and truth. Rather, it is believed that such standards are imminent within scholarly and other practices. Second, the thesis of the unity of science is questioned. The main image of science, as either formally demonstrative or empirically compelling, "relates poorly to actual practices in science that historians, sociologists, psychologists, and (increasingly) rhetoricians . . . have uncovered" (Nelson & Megill 1986, p. 23). Third is the rhetorical conception of epistemology. Rhetoric is epistemic: it produces and shapes knowledge, rather than being a mere tool in the communication of messages.

The rhetoric of inquiry has two important messages for psychology, the first on the level of theorizing and the second on the object level. On the level of theorizing, the message contains a critique of the dominant belief in a fixed logic of inquiry. "Rhetoric of inquiry studies research as continuing argument within disciplines. It explores inquiries as networks of cases, stories, metaphors, measurements, experiments, seminars, and publications. On one side, it means more subtle and sympathetic attention by philosophers of science to aspects of discovery, meaning, persuasion, and sociology that were earlier scorned as nonlogical. On another side, it includes psychological studies of human inference . . ." (Nelson & Megill, p. 31). Traditional methodologies, insofar as they use an idealized picture of the natural sciences to guide research in the social sciences, provide rhetoric *about* inquiry. By contrast, the rhetoric *of* inquiry is concerned with rhetoric as it is actually practiced. This is not meant to contrast rhetoric with rationality: "the need is to recognize that rhetoric is reasonable and reason is rhetorical" (Nelson & Megill, p. 33). The contributions to the volume edited by Nelson, Megill & McCloskey, *The Rhetoric of the Human Sciences* (1987), approach various disciplines from this vantage point.

Second, on the object level of psychology the message of rhetoric is that social life has important argumentative aspects. In the words of

Michael Billig, whose *Arguing and Thinking* (1987) is a forceful example of the rhetorical approach in psychology, "arguments are such a constant theme in the history of social rules, (that) their psychological importance should be recognized. However, psychologists will be unable to give due attention to argumentation so long as they employ theoretical frameworks which subtract the argumentative aspects from human activities" (1987, p. 30). Billig has demonstrated the neglect of argumentative aspects in the frequently used metaphors of life as a game and life as theatre -- the latter e.g. in its influential cognitive version of script theory (p. 13 ff.). In short, a rhetorical approach stresses the two-sidedness of human thinking and of our conceptual capacities (p. 49) and the importance of dialogue, which is often characterized by the 'spirit of contradiction'. This leads to different expectations concerning the object world under investigation. Instead of a fixed eternal world, as Plato envisioned the world of ideas, or a world governed by laws of nature that are waiting to be discovered, the "world of rhetoric is a less certain world" (Billig, p. 48).

In the following sections, I will look at various theories about dreaming, trying to understand their rhetorics. I will especially try to show how certain preconceptions about the nature of knowledge and rationality shape the form and contents of theories. Not merely metaphors for the objects of research, methodologies also exert powerful influences on individual researchers and whole disciplines (which may be seen as tribes with shared rules and convictions). They determine what one is allowed to see, say, write about, and research. But first something must be said about the object level: dreaming. How do dreams function rhetorically? Does dreaming show the argumentative structure that Michael Billig presumes in human thought, talk, and action? This forms the subject of the next section.

2. *The Dream in Modern Psychology*

In his stimulating book *The Innocence of Dreams*, Charles Rycroft concludes that dreams are best understood if one forgets all theories about them and ceases to think of them as discrete items of experience. Instead, one might respond to them as glimpses of the dreamer's total imaginative fabric; but it takes some effort before one has succeeded in overcoming major Western stereotypes (often defended in the form of scientific hypotheses). To the cultured and scientifically-minded, dreams are bizarre, chaotic, nonsensical, and meaningless whereas in a more popular folklore dreams are bizarre, mysterious and meaningfully though cryptically related to the future.

Modern theories about dream interpretation are dominated by Freudian conceptions, whether they agree with Freud or not. One of Freud's most influential ideas was the distinction he made between primary and secondary processes. The dream is a major example of primary process thinking, along with mythical thought and the creation of art. Freud must be credited for the importance he attached to this underestimated side of our thought in his theorizing. But he combined his interest in visual and non-conceptual thought with a peculiar characterization of it as regressive and archaic.

It has taken some time before psychoanalysts became aware that there is really no justification for regarding dream thought as regressive, infantile, or archaic. In the past decades, however, important studies have appeared that emphasize primary process thought as a mode of mentation in its own right (Fosshage 1983, Noy 1969). Fosshage, who is especially concerned with the function of dreams, rejects the biologically-based drive-discharge model. Instead, he views dreams as adaptive and restorative, as attempts to integrate current cognitive and affective experiences through the development of new structures and the resolution of conflicts. Dreams are particularly suited for these purposes because they are in the primary process mode: they use visual and other sensory images with intense affective colorations for their integrative work. From this point of view, one can still speak of displacement in dreams, but it is no longer seen as merely a form of concealment (such as Freud's drive-discharge model would have it). "Displacement is conceived of here as an organizing principle in which experiences generating the same affective reaction ... are all nodal points or cues for a particular thematic experience" (Fosshage 1983, p. 650-1). The nodal point usually expresses a poignant affective thematic experience.

In line with this rehabilitation of primary process, those concerned with the interpretation of dreams have drawn attention to the manifest dream - which is in the primary process mode, contrary to a popular misunderstanding - and its comprehensibility in itself (Spanjaard 1969, 1988; Ehebald 1980; Bartels 1979). Dreaming is conceptualized as a foreign language which one must learn to understand. For those who have mastered this language, the rough meaning of many dreams may be clear without the need of much context. Before one is able to establish the precise meaning of the dream for the dreamer, it remains necessary to know the context of the individual life in which it was dreamt. A dream is a highly private affair, using a lot of personal meanings, since it is not meant, after all, to explain something to others by means of conventional language. The interplay between the dream language and the individual context is what we can learn to understand (Wijngaarden 1985).

There is no doubt that this modern psychoanalytic notion of the dream, perhaps formulated first by ego-psychologists like Erich Fromm (1951) and French and Fromm (1964), comes much closer to Jung's method of dream interpretation than Freud would have liked (see Jung 1934/1974, 1984).

Rycroft (1979), who is a former psychoanalyst, rejects most of Freud's assumptions in dream theory, which he regards as dogmatic and heavily burdened by theoretical speculation. As I indicated at the beginning of this section, he aims at a more practical, down-to-earth approach to dream interpretation, trying to forget all kinds of theoretical garbage. In one respect he still reminds me of analytical theories: he thinks of people consisting of different agencies trying to communicate (p. 52).[1] For Jung, the agent who sends messages in dreams is the Personal, but also the Collective Unconscious; for Freud, the (non-)communications are between conscious and unconscious, or, in his later model, between Ego, Id, and Superego. Rycroft stands in this tradition, for he regards dreams as messages from parts of ourselves to other parts of ourselves. The dreaming self is clearly not exactly the same as the waking self that remembers the dream - hence the difficulties in understanding. The waking self tends to disclaim responsibility for the dream. Yet, it tells something about him or her, about what Freud called the unconscious, or the Id, in a metaphorical language full of private meanings and images. And so the dreamer is concerned with an internal rhetorical process, directed against his own convictions and arguments. I don't think this need be taken as a manifestation of homunculi or different selves: I am trying to describe the structure of a peculiar form of thinking, somewhat in the same way that Billig (1987) has described forms of daily thought as rhetorical arguments. Bert States (1988) has described dreams from a different perspective as narratives organized by the four master tropes: metonymy, synecdoche, metaphor, and irony. This could be viewed as a more detailed and nuanced description of the same transformations that Kuper (1979, 1986) notices in dreams. Kuper derives his idea from Lévi-Strauss's structural analysis of myth: likewise, dreams are shown to constitute a set of systematic transformations of a single structure. The structure contains a number of oppositions that represent a dilemma or conflict facing the dreamer. So dreams are seen as rhetorical modes of argument in which a problem is resolved by a series of orderly transformations of a given, concrete initial situation.

Second, Rycroft maintains that dreaming is "an activity of which we are inevitably to an extent innocent, partly because there is more to the imagination than any individual moment of consciousness can apprehend, and partly because it bears a relationship to conscious selfhood analogous to that of the Wind to the Windhover it sustains in flight - omnipresent and yet not in its particularities perceptible" (1979, p. 168-9). This so-called 'innocence' is another characteristic of dreams which has been widely recognized. The narratives develop in their own way, according to rules of their own. This is even true for those who have learned to be conscious while dreaming, and are able to make choices and steer their dreams to an extent (Tholey 1986, Tholey & Utecht 1988). There are still things beyond their control. Lucid dreamers are only better able to respond to the unexpected than the average 'unconscious' dreamer.

Seen in this way, dreams become products of the imagination comparable to poems, paintings, and novels; the major difference being that art usually draws upon generally accessible symbols and metaphors. A dream, on the other hand, requires that we dive into the personality and history of the dreamer to get some clarity. Once we do this, of course, very soon we have not found just one meaning, but several meanings of each dream: it is not easy to stop because we never hit rockbottom. This is not an uncommon situation in psychology, as Kenneth Gergen has shown in various instances (see chapter 4). Gergen et al. (1986) have given interesting examples of the open-endedness of psychological descriptions of personality. This multitude of meanings scares many scientists away.[2] Indeed, one is free to deny the meaning of things, and one may argue that nothing valuable can result from the study of phenomena whose order of reality is so ill-defined. As Rycroft puts it, "the first and most obvious similarity between dreams and products of the literary imagination is that they can be granted or refused meaning according to the predilection of the person who has, hears or reads them" (p. 162). Rycroft goes on to say this is obvious in the case of dreams, but that it is less obvious that it is possible to deny meaning to poems and novels.

The denial of meaning is practiced by many psychologists within the context of their research. Though they may be avid readers of novels and poetry in their spare time, academic psychologists are inclined to argue that poems are not accessible to scientific research and are therefore meaningless in so far as their theories are concerned. Up to a point this is unobjectionable. In chapter 1 I have argued that the empirical-analytical method may be applied to any realm of human reality, as long as it remains clear that it cannot grasp internal relations as such. For those who wish to study the regularities in the external relations between variables, the empirical-analytical method is appropriate. Later I have pointed out that those like A. Grünbaum (see chapter 5), who regard the empirical-analytical method as the only approach to reality yielding real knowledge, are really defending a scientistic world view, an ontology resting on shaky epistemological grounds. In this regard, the scientific study of dreams presents a nice occasion to observe the application of the empirical-analytical method in actual practice. My aim in this chapter is to present some examples of scientific approaches to dreams, coming from fields like neurophysiology and cognitive psychology, in order to analyze their hypotheses and conclusions from a rhetorical vantage point. As I hope to make clear, the empirical-analytical approach is encapsulated in a series of rhetorical devices that go beyond the objective study of variables. Second, I hope that this analysis of current theories may shed some light on the phenomena themselves. As I have already indicated, I believe that it is a fruitful approach to dreams to view them as an independent form of thinking with a rhetorical structure.

3. *Neurophysiological Reductionism: The Activation-Synthesis Hypothesis of the Dream Process*

In an influential article, Hobson & McCarley (1977) have suggested that the formal characteristics of the dream process (such as 'bizarreness') may be the result of the specific way the brain works during our dreaming. On the basis of new neurophysiological evidence they criticize Freud's theory of dreams. I say 'suggested' instead of 'argued' because their argument is not absolutely clear on all points, a matter that will be explained in the course of my critical reaction to their conclusions. My point will be to show that Hobson & McCarley present their evidence in a way that may superficially look convincing to adherents of an empiricist view of science, but miss the point really, because they are drawing upon old-fashioned clichés about dreaming in the course of their article. It is thanks to these clichés that they have found an audience. In the following, I will concentrate on the article mentioned because it is most widely known and has influenced several other theoretists. In 1988, Hobson's book *The Dreaming Brain* appeared, in which essentially the same theses are defended, though the argument is expanded considerably. Later on I will make a few points concerning the book.

What exactly is the evidence Hobson & McCarley draw upon and what are their assumptions? We may note two assumptions. The first assumption is that a mind-body isomorphism exists, a similarity of form between neurophysiological events during dreaming and the formal aspects of the dream process, seen as a mental experience, characterized by hallucinoid imagery, bizarre elements, and a delusional acceptance of these phenomena as 'real' at the time they occur. The second assumption is that dreams (at least 'real' hallucinatory dreams) occur only during the phase known as D-sleep (desynchronized sleep, also known as REM-sleep).

Starting from these assumptions, Hobson & McCarley formulate several hypotheses. The first hypothesis is that dreams are solely generated by random stimulation from the pontine brain stem, a part of the brain which functions both as trigger and as clock of dreaming. Second, the formal characteristics of dreams (with the term 'formal', Hobson & McCarley refer to what they call the 'bizarreness' and 'distortion' of dreams) are caused by random stimulation of the forebrain by the pons. Third, in so far as we find a coherent narrative structure (or meaning) in dreams, it must be caused by the synthesizing activity of the forebrain. Fourth, as a conclusion from the first three hypotheses, Hobson & McCarley maintain that the dream is not determined by ideas, but solely by the pontine reticular formation, "the site of an executive or triggering mechanism for desynchronized sleep .... If we assume that the physiological substrate of consciousness is in the forebrain, these facts completely eliminate any possible contribution of ideas (or their neural substrate) to the primary driving force of the dream process" (Hobson & McCarley 1977, p. 1338). Fifth, on the basis of the above, they criticize Freud, who maintained that dreaming occurs to protect sleep from the disruptive effect of unconscious wishes that are released in sleep. Dreaming occurs periodically during the night when the pontine brain stem randomly activates the forebrain, which makes "the best of a bad job in producing even partially coherent dream imagery from the relatively noisy signals" (p. 1347), taking care of a synthesis. Hence the name, Activation-Synthesis Hypothesis.

The activation-synthesis hypothesis has been criticized both on methodological grounds and on the basis of contrary neurobiological evidence. I draw upon the arguments presented by Vogel (1978) in his critique of Hobson & McCarley, going through the assumptions and theses listed earlier. First, the assumption of mind-body isomorphism must remain an entirely philosophical statement. From a philosophical viewpoint of mind-body dualism, it seems plausible that every mental event has a physiological correlate. Indeed, this has been argued on several grounds and in various forms by so-called "Mind/Brain Identity Theorists" (see Borst, 1970). I don't want to enter this philosophical discussion. I just want to point out that the philosophical thesis that it is possible to think that a perfect mind-body isomorphism (or even identity) has a status basically different from any empirical claims about correlations between thoughts and neuronal activity. This is what Hobson & McCarley don't seem to realize. They present empirical claims which seem to be based only on the assumption of isomorphism. As Vogel argues, "we do not know the neural correlates of particular sequences of mentation .... our ignorance about these issues is very great. In view of such ignorance, the claim that disordered (incoherent) meaning is caused by disordered (random) discharge of individual pontine cells appears to be based on verbal similarity rather than empirical findings" (Vogel 1978, p. 1532).

As to the second assumption, it is simply not true that dreaming is limited to the D-state. During sleep onset, awakenings from non-D-state stages result in a high frequency (50%-70%) of dream reports. These sleep onset dreams are quite similar to D-state dreams in bizarreness, length, and dreamlike quality (see Vogel, p. 1534).

We may then turn to the first hypothesis of Hobson & McCarley: dreams are solely generated by pontine FTG cells. On the basis of evidence reviewed by Vogel, we can conclude that this thesis must be rejected on empirical grounds. The evidence indicates that "the forebrain plays a crucial role in the instigation, maintenance and timing of most episodes of D-sleep" (p. 1532).

The second hypothesis concerned formal characteristics of dreams such as dream distortion, held to be caused by a partially random discharge of neuronal units in the pontine D-state generator. As Vogel argues, it is entirely without empirical support; there are however relevant studies which speak contrary to the hypothesis. "Furthermore, based on the high frequency of random phasic bursts of the generator, the hypothesis would predict that distortion, bizarreness, and incoherence are very frequent characteristics of dreams. However, D-state dreams usually contain realistic imagery, concern banal everyday events, and display remarkable thematic coherence . . . D-state dreams simply do not resemble that kaleidoscopic barrage of unconnected images one would expect from a random generator of mentation" (p. 1532).

Third hypothesis: "The elaboration of the brain stem stimulus by the perceptual, conceptual and emotional structures of the forebrain is viewed as primarily a synthetic constructive process . . . The brain, in the dreaming sleep state, is thus likened to a computer searching its addresses for key words" (Hobson & McCarley 1977, p. 1347). The reply to this hypothesis must be that it involves such explanatory agility that it becomes empirically meaningless. As Vogel puts it, "the activation-synthesis hypothesis cannot explain the remarkable coherence of most dreams by shifting its emphasis from the disordering effect of random hindbrain stimulation to the ordering effect of a forebrain synthesizing response. Such an explanation would mean that although the hypothesis has not predicted dream coherence, it could, post hoc, conveniently invoke just the right amount of synthetic activity to explain the observed coherence of any dream" (p. 1532). It seems that we can discard the third hypothesis as another version of mind/body isomorphism with the appearance of specified empirical contents, but actually no empirical meaning at all.

We have then arrived at the fourth hypothesis: dreams are determined by pontine brain cells, rather than by ideas. It is worth looking again at the precise formulations by Hobson & McCarley: "The primary motivating force for dreaming is not psychological but physiological .... Specific stimuli for the dream imagery appear to arise intracerebrally but from the pontine brain stem and not in cognitive areas of the cerebrum. .... The dream process is thus seen as having its origin in sensorimotor systems, with little or no primary ideational, volitional, or emotional content .... Thus both the major energetic drive for the dream process and the specific primary stimulus of the dream content are genotypically determined and therefore conflict free ...." (p. 1346-7).

Two reactions to these propositions are possible, one from an empirical point of view, the other methodological. Starting with the former, the reader will perhaps remember how Vogel argued that the forebrain is also necessary for the instigation, maintenance, and timing of most D-sleep episodes. Apart from that, correlational evidence contradicts the claim that the formal characteristics of dreams are related to phasic pontine activation. Vogel concludes that "the evidence does not support the crux of the hypothesis, that (pontine) physiological processes rather than psychological processes instigate dreams and determine their formal characteristics" (Vogel 1978, p. 1534).

The methodological reaction stands quite apart from the arguments given so far. It states more radically that the evidence *can* not, for logical reasons, support the crux of the hypothesis. Turning to the quotations from Hobson & McCarley presented above, it could be said that they play on the ambiguity of the words used. A "primary motivating force" is psychological, not physiological, unless a cause is meant: but then it cannot be psychological. A "major energetic drive" is necessarily "conflict-free" in the psychodynamic sense: how could physiological energy be conflict-ridden? It seems that Hobson & McCarley are as much trapped by neurological metaphors as Freud sometimes was.

Vogel has formulated the methodological critique clearly: "neurophysiological variables cannot be used to test a psychological theory of dreams (such as Freud's) when the correlation between the relevant psychological variables and the relevant phsyiological variables is unknown" (p. 1534). It is unknown and will remain unknown in the near future, if not forever. "Furthermore, even when the relevant psycho-physiological correlations are known, the use of physiological variables provides only an indirect test of the theory" (ibid).

We have then arrived at the fifth and last hypothesis: Freud's theory of the dream as a guardian of sleep is criticized. This theory has been abandoned by many psychoanalysts and other dream interpreters on psychological grounds. Though it seems reasonable to doubt the defensive function of all dreams, this is not because of physiological evidence. It remains possible that certain physiological stimuli embody 'forbidden wishes' on the Freudian psychological level.

In conclusion, Hobson & McCarley have failed to demonstrate that the psychology of dreaming has something to learn from neurophysiology. Instead, they have given a demonstration of reductionism.

I have dealt with the Activation-Synthesis Theory so extensively because it forms an example of a theory which suggests psychological relevance by an ambiguous use of terms. It uses the language of neurophysiology as a rhetorical weapon in psychology. Hobson covers much of the same ground in his book *The Dreaming Brain* (1988), where he amazes the reader again with his confusion between the levels of dream experiences and neurological occurrences. But here he has found a place to expound his own views on dream interpretation, an activity he considers important for clinical practice. His rejection of the Freudian wish-fulfillment theory, with the notions of censorship and disguise, is entirely in line with modern psychoanalytic criticisms as we have encountered earlier in Fosshage (1983). Hobson seems to be unaware of this, since he never mentions the recent literature. This lends a rather naive character to his ideas on dream interpretation. He wants to convince the reader that dreams are transparent. In so far as this means that dreams are not the result of unconscious wishes and censorship, many would agree with him. But if he wishes to claim that the meaning of dreams is obvious to anyone not indoctrinated by psychoanalysis, he makes himself hard to believe. Theorists from various non-Freudian origins still tend to disagree on the meaning of dreams (see Fosshage & Loew 1978). This shouldn't surprise us, first of all because different theoretical assumptions still determine interpretations, but also because it is usually necessary to situate a dream in the highly individual context in which it was dreamt before we can understand it fully. This is a complex task, leading to many possibilities of interpretation. Hobson nowhere presents arguments against this view, unless he thinks his assertion that certain examples of dreams are fully understandable to him, and *thus* transparent, counts as an argument. What he would have to do (being a scientist, and very keen on experimenting, as he depicts himself) is to present many dreams to many interpreters (trained in activation-synthesis theory, of course) and observe whether consensus emerges. That would mean a real test, and it could provide evidence for Hobson's views.

With these few remarks, I cannot do justice to Hobson's book. I maintain, however, that all the arguments against the Activation-

Synthesis Hypothesis apply as much to Hobson's most recent work as to the earlier articles. Before turning to a theory inspired by the Activation-Synthesis Hypothesis, a few remarks need to be made on the notion of isomorphism.

Isomorphism

With the argument as presented above, I'm not suggesting that the study of the neurobiological basis of dreaming could not be relevant to the interpretation of dreams. I am curious to learn in what way, but I don't think we have to assume that biological phenomena are ontologically prior to psychological and cultural phenomena. It could as well be the other way round, even though that sounds outrageous to many scientists and is not a popular thing to believe at this moment. Parisi (1987) is one of the few psychologists to challenge the widely- spread assumption about the primary nature of biology.

Generally speaking, the argument for reductionism is rather loose and boils down to the assumption that there is some kind of isomorphism between different levels, such as the language of physiology and the level of psychological motives and ideas. As we have seen, it is sometimes thought that concepts from one level are metaphorically applicable to the other level. Even when we regard the study of the cellular and molecular basis of the sleep cycle as a promising field of research (cf. Hobson et al, 1986), we can question the use of metaphors independently.

Many problems in psychology are tackled with analogies, models borrowed from related disciplines, and metaphors. An example is formed by the digital computer as a model for human thought, or alternatively the connectionist model of parallel processes (Wolters & Phaf 1988). There is an interesting feature of this recent research which may be relevant to the problem of isomorphism. Scientists have become used to the uncertainty principle in quantum mechanics. A deterministic world view is neither necessary nor adequate in some parts of science. Undeterministic 'chaos' on one level may result in predictable processes on another.[3]

The same situation seems to exist in other fields as well. Meteorologists believe in a deterministic level of macroscopic events that determine the weather. At least from 1919 on, they know reasonably well how to explain these events in scientific models. Yet in regard to weather forecasts in the intermediate to long range, they have come to the conclusion that the weather is an essentially unpredictable process because of its 'chaotic' features (Tribbia et al 1987).

Another example is the assumption made in connectionist theory that brains create chaos in order to make sense of the world (Skarda & Freeman 1987). In short, chaos on one level of description may be necessary or at least compatible with deterministic processes on another level. It seems to me that this realization might be relevant for the construction of models about dreaming. For instance, learning new behavior could benefit by 'chaotic' or rule-defying thought processes in dreaming. Something like this has been suggested by Liam Hudson (1984) in *Nightlife*: he argues that we may benefit from our dreams in divergent thinking. Creative people usually remember more dreams than those normally engaged in convergent thought.

4. *Visual Bursts, Cognitive Synthesis, and the Meaning of Dreams*

Seligman & Yellen (1987) have proposed an interesting new theory of dream construction which, in their opinion, has consequences for the interpretation of dreams. I will sketch the basic outlines of this theory and then investigate whether it indeed possesses relevance for the meaning of dreams. Seligman & Yellen look upon dreaming as a partly rhetorical activity; the dreamer in the role of a director preserving coherence in the play by cognitive elaboration of the primary visual elements of each scene. But as I will argue, their use of the metaphor of the theater is only partial: without sound reasons, they leave all that happens backstage to physiology, as if it doesn't belong to human thought and action.

Dreaming, according to Seligman & Yellen, consists of three elements: periodic, unrelated visual bursts, emotional episodes, and the cognitive synthesis of the first two. The visual bursts account for the vivid and detailed visual imagery in dreams. In contrast, the cognitive elaboration of the bursts and emotions is less vivid and detailed. This difference has a physiological basis, to be explained below. Another difference between the two kinds of visual imagery is that the bursts are unexpected: the dreamer experiences them passively, whereas the cognitive synthesis is an active process, comparable to constructing a narrative around a series of pictures. Thus, the unexpected vivid events in dreams must be visual bursts, and may be expected to be less constrained by the plot of the dream (narrative) than the less vivid cognitive episodes.

Seligman & Yellen indicate three sources of inspiration for their hypotheses. First, the well-known phenomenon that we actively impose order on that which is unpatterned. Second, within the phase of D-sleep or Rapid Eye Movement (REM) sleep, two components have been distinguished (e.g. by Pivik, 1978): the REM stage consists of phasic activity, superimposed on tonic REM activity. The REM bout is made up of periodic bursts of REM lasting about 2 - 9 seconds alternating with REM quiescences each lasting about 16-120 sec. There has been some research into these phases, but the findings have remained contradictory and inconclusive (Seligman & Yellen 1987, p. 2). In any case, Seligman & Yellen reopen the discussion on a psychological level by suggesting that visual bursts and cognitive elaborations are different substages which may be recognized in every dream. Third, the activation-synthesis model of Hobson & McCarley, dealt with in the last section, is used as a clue. Seligman & Yellen call their own theory "a psychological version of the physiological theory of Hobson & McCarley" (p. 3). As we have seen earlier, these authors assume the brainstem triggers forebrain activity, without the forebrain influencing brainstem activity. Likewise, Seligman & Yellen assume visual bursts are not influenced by cognitive synthesis; these events appear periodically, are unrelated, are passively witnessed by the dreamer, and not meaningful. Only during cognitive elaboration is meaning created. "None of the three elements that we postulate influence what the content of the next visual hallucination will be", Seligman & Yellen write (p. 3).

Seligman & Yellen maintain that the cognitive synthesis is an attempt to integrate, explain, make sense of, and synthesize the visual bursts with the emotional episodes -- in other words, to actively construct a coherent plot. From this, they deduct that there should be two distinguishable systems of visual information in a dream, a vivid and a less vivid one. This hypothesis is tested experimentally. Furthermore, it is postulated that the meaning of dreams can be found in the cognitive synthesis. "We believe that understanding how cognitive integration takes place will provide the rules for finding meaning in a dream ... we do not find it [meaning] in the content of the visual bursts" (p. 22).

In my reaction to the theory of Seligman & Yellen, I will focus on this statement about the meaning of dreams. First, I will ask whether it is possible to isolate visual bursts unproblematically from within a dream narrative. Second, assuming for the sake of argument that visual bursts may be recognized phenomenologically or from the analysis of a dream narrative, is it true they are not meaningful and unrelated to earlier parts of the dream? Isn't the clue from Hobson & McCarley misleading in this respect? Finally, I will argue that 'passive' experiences can be meaningful and show how the metaphor of the theater may be expanded to make it more adequate in its application to dream thought.

Recognition of visual bursts

Suppose that Seligman & Yellen correctly assume that visual bursts occur on the physiological level. How can we identify these bursts in actual dreams? In the first place, a dreamer can indicate what he regards as the most vivid visual experiences in the dream, as distinct from more thought-like images. This is a phenomenological identification. Second, we can try to analyze any given dream narrative and look for unexpected elements that do not cohere very well with the plot of the dream. This could be called a descriptive identification. Seligman & Yellen assume that these identifications are relatively unproblematic. In a series of dreams presented in their article, the bursts are described without much argument. Since the dreams (12 in all) seem to be Seligman's (this is not made explicit), the method of identification used would be phenomenological. Then it would make sense that no arguments are given. In a small experiment designed to find out how easy it is to recognize visual bursts when reading a dream, I presented dream no. 10 (Seligman & Yellen, p. 18: "I was in the car with my family ...") to five students. They counted much more bursts than the three indicated by Seligman & Yellen: totals ranged from 4 to 13. The number of scenes (Seligman & Yellen: 3) was usually held to be 4, with one subject insisting on 7. This suggests at least that it is not easy to explain what the concept "visual burst" means.

Seligman & Yellen test their hypothesis concerning visual bursts in an experiment. "The theory uniquely predicts that the *most vivid images in a dream should be those images that are the least constrained by what has already occurred in the plot.* That is, the vivid images should be the surprising images in the dream. Images that are less clear, vague, or fuzzy are generated by the cognitive integration, and should be more continuous with the plot" (Seligman & Yellen, p. 7). In order to test this hypothesis, subjects were asked to report a dream from last night in detail, according to the instruction to *only* "report a dream that had a *sequence* of three or more events, and report them in the order that they happened".

The results confirmed the hypothesis: in a majority of cases, the most vivid images turned out to be the most surprising. But we need not be surprised by this. It seems that the method of data collection was highly biased. Only dreams that had a sequence of three or more events were taken into consideration. This means that there was a strong pressure on the subjects to describe their dreams as consisting of separate events, even when they normally would have told a different story. Dreams not easily split into elements were not reported at all. The next question was to "take the four or five most vivid images in your dream and rank order them", and to list "one or two images in your dream that were vague or unclear".

Now, on purely common sense grounds it seems plausible to me that the latter images were later judged to be the least surprising ones. This doesn't seem to provide evidence for the unrelatedness of visual bursts in dreams.

But although this experiment may be inconclusive, the hypothesis about visual bursts it was meant to test is intriguing. I have therefore devised another method of investigation. The results of this research are not yet available. What especially deserves attention, in my opinion, is the problem whether visual bursts are identifiable at all. The methodological critique of Hobson & McCarley may apply here as well: the existence of physiological bursts with definite characteristics does not imply that similar structures will be found on the phenomenological level or in dream narratives. To mention only one obvious problem, in order to identify visual stimuli we need concepts; in every observation, however passive it may be, we are engaged in a cognitive synthesis. So the distinction between passive visual experiences and active cognitive synthesis may well turn out to be an idealization with no pragmatic value.

The theater metaphor

The metaphor of the theater has been frequently used in psychology. Well-known is the script theory of Schank and Abelson, who assume that the action of the play (c.q. social behavior) is usually determined by a script ("a predetermined, stereotyped sequence of actions that defines a well-known situation"). Michael Billig has criticized this and other uses of the dramaturgical metaphor on the ground that it only partially covers the world. "In particular, the dramaturgical metaphor only presents a view of the theatrical world from which the argumentative aspects have been removed .... It narrows the world of the theatre down to the staged performance. If all the world is a stage, then what goes on backstage is being excluded" (Billig 1987, p. 15). What Billig wants to show is that the public performance, as a more or less script-determined series of actions, is only made possible by backstage preparations and arguments which are characteristically less determined. Backstage there is the possibility of argument. This important aspect of human action is suppressed by the metaphor of the theater.

I want to apply this idea now to the theory of Seligman & Yellen. This theory reduces the dream, in so far as it is understandable, to a series of consistent cognitive acts, each enhancing the coherence and intelligibility of the dream. The visual bursts, as disruptive elements, are deprived of meaning, being random, physiologically determined, passively witnessed, and not constrained internally. This leads Seligman & Yellen to hypotheses about dream interpretation - it certainly forms an interesting aspect of their article that they offer a theory of dream construction with potential relevance for the interpretation of dreams. The twelve dreams used as illustrations for the formation of dream narratives are partially investigated as to their meaning at the same time. In their own words, "this leads us to the best candidate for the locus of meaning: the way we integrate the visual bursts with the emotional setting ... We believe that understanding how cognitive integration takes place will provide the rules for finding meaning in a dream .... If we seek for meaning ... we do not find it in the content of the visual bursts" (p. 22).

This conclusion sounds surprising with regard to the external constraints on the content of visual bursts mentioned earlier: Seligman & Yellen speak of 'unconscious conflicts' and 'day residues' (p. 20). After discussing the problem of recurring dreams, they formulate a weak version of the thesis: "this theory suggests that the visual bursts are *not necessarily* pregnant with meaning" (p. 21, my emphasis). This, of course, undermines their rule for dream interpretation quoted earlier. It seems that it is very difficult to maintain that (1) dreams contain unambiguously identifiable elements, which are (2) not meaningful.

Indeed, if we look at narratives in general, are we surprised to learn that they contain a certain amount of unexpected and surprising elements? A narrative is never a logical sequence of deductions from a set of axioms given in the first scene: coherence can exist even when new events and ideas are introduced at various places in the narrative. I have never heard a literary theorist arguing that such new elements are deprived of meaning. Seen from this perspective, the fact that dreams consist of surprising episodes and contain bizarre ideas at most shows a difference of degree with other forms of thought and narrative.[4]

I conclude that the relevance of research into the construction of dreams for dream interpretation remains to be demonstrated. Seligman & Yellen have unfortunately repeated the mistake of Hobson & McCarley in their attempt to reduce psychology to brain neurology.

Remaining on the psychological level, it seems to be advisable to use metaphors that include human argumentation and defiance of fixed rules. Isn't this exactly what dreaming is? From a rhetorical point of view, dreaming is indeed a form of thought where there is an excellent opportunity of denying the validity of existing rules. The physiological suppression of motor activity in dreaming phases allows dreamers an unlimited freedom of the imagination.

5. *The "unlearning" hypothesis: Dreaming in order to forget*

Crick & Mitchison have argued that the function of dream sleep could be to remove certain undesirable modes of interaction in networks of cells in the cerebral cortex. They postulate that this is done in REM sleep by a 'reverse learning mechanism', so that the trace in the brain of the unconscious dream is weakened, rather than strengthened by the dream. In certain neuronal networks, described by Crick & Mitchinson (1983, 1986), similar behavior will occur if the net is overloaded: "(1) The net may produce many far-fetched or bizarre associations ('fantasy'). (2) The net may tend to produce the same state ... whatever the input ('obsession'). (3) Certain kinds of nets ... may respond to inappropriate input signals which would normally evoke no response from the net ('hallucination')" (p. 112). Now, of course, some mechanism is needed to dampen these 'potentially parasitic modes'. "Such a rough outline description immediately reminds one of REM-sleep and the hallucinoid dreams associated with it" (C & M 1983, p. 112).

These analogies make Crick and Mitchison think that in REM-sleep we unlearn our unconscious dreams. "We dream in order to forget." After reverse learning in our sleep, our thinking may become less confused. Thanks to our cleaning-up mechanism to remove potentially parasitic modes, we are able to survive. Indeed, "attempting to remember one's dreams should perhaps not be encouraged, because such remembering may help to retain patterns of thought which are better forgotten" (Crick & Mitchison 1983, p. 114).[5]

This argument sounds very coherent and convincing, but one question remains.

How do we -- or Crick and Mitchison, for that matter -- know that our dreams, of all forms of thought, contain patterns which are better forgotten? Why are Crick and Mitchison so irresistably reminded of "parasitic modes of behavior", when they think of dreams? It seems that they know at least something about dreams: dream narratives, in their eyes, are incomprehensible. But one wonders about their grounds for this belief. Is it ignorance? Could it be a common sense preconception? In a later article, Crick & Mitchison (1986) explain their reluctance to say something about the meaning of dreams: there is no consensus in the field of dream interpretation, so it is better to avoid it until we know more about the physiological mechanisms underlying dreaming. And so the circle closes. The physiological theory rests on cliches about dreaming derived from (scientific) folklore (Crick and Mitchison, again, are inspired by the ideas of Hobson & McCarley). Scientific folklore holds that dreams are irrational. Instead of studying this preconception as a tentative hypothesis, scientific models are constructed that explain the function of these 'irrational' modes of thought.

This theory about the function of dream sleep, in short, is convincing only for those who start from the belief that dreams are irrational parasitic modes of thought. Led by similar methodological, 'scientific' motives, Freud regarded his self-discovered primary process thought as archaic, regressive, and non-adaptive. As indicated in section 2 above, the primary process has been rehabilitated by modern analysts and dream theoreticians as a potentially creative, imaginative, and adaptive form of mentation. Crick and Mitchison have failed to show that this view is unpromising: they have just felt that it may lead to ambiguity, different views on possible meanings, and a lack of consensus. And this cannot be denied: these are the essential features of man's rhetorical nature. Moreover, it sounds conceivable that people may 'unlearn', by the use of method, the capacities of imagination, creativity, and negative capability. Whether this is desirable is another matter.

6. *Dream Interpretation and the Imagination*

I began this chapter with a consideration of the rhetorical nature both of the object of psychology and psychological theorizing. In the last sections I have tried to show the curious effects of an objectivistic denial of the rhetorical nature of dreams. It seems that theoretical progress is hampered by clinging too much to abstract ideals of rational thought. Some of the most objective approaches to dreams are fraught with grave empirical and methodological problems. The objectivity they claim seems to be used as a rhetorical device in the first place. An interesting feature shared by the three theories is that the objectivity on the methodological theorizing level seems to determine the characteristics of dreams found (or postulated) at the object level. We might speak of "methodomorphism" using Danziger's (1985) term. Apparently, the methodological imperative (see chapter 1) restrains the possibilities for observation and theorizing.

In itself, it is not surprising that dream experiences are difficult to understand from the point of view of neurophysiology. Dreams are traditionally associated with ambiguity, the imagination, and the uncanny. For those who start off from rationalist assumptions, the dream must seem the literal opposite of rationality: it appears to be irrational, rule-breaking, abnormal, nonsensical, anti-logical, immature, insane, regressive, subjective, and incomprehensible.

Instead, in literary disciplines the character of the dream is not so easily considered outrageous. If I am right, the adequate perspective for looking at dream thought is not provided by the metaphor of language as a mirror of nature. In empirical-analytical methodology, theories are viewed as reflections of reality. I hope the preceding pages have thrown enough doubts on this assumption. Freud put his modern objectivistic stance - which forms at least one aspect of his thought - in a recommendation to analysts, when he said that "the physician should be impenetrable to the patient, and, like a mirror, reflect nothing but what is shown to him" (1912e, p. 118). Whole generations of analysts have vainly tried to conform to this ideal, before it became clear that such an attitude has severe practical drawbacks and is an impossibility in any case.[6] For even in science, theories and concepts are not simply mirrors of reality; they create reality, they determine the way we experience the world. To understand dreams, one might think of modern art, not of paintings or photographs that aim to represent the world accurately. Likewise, in post-modern literary criticism, the notion of the novel as a portrait of reality is questioned. To give just one example, "the ambivalence of *Ulysses* precludes the possibility of reading it as the mirror of a stable, unified reality outside itself. There is no single origin outside the text to anchor and fix its meaning, since the idea of origin was erased as the verbal cosmos came into existence" (Van Boheemen 1987, p. 170). The dream may be regarded as an experience that might sensitize us for this cosmos with its ambiguous and imaginative aspects, and enhance our negative capability. Dreaming stages 'the other'. Might not psychology draw its inspiration more from the arts and traditional humanities and expect less from the sciences?

No doubt: this is a rhetorical question.

NOTES

Introduction

1. The term "hermeneutics" will be used here as a common name for various interpretative approaches. "Empirical-hermeneutical approaches" is a bit too long, though the term has the distinct advantage to preclude the misunderstanding that hermeneutical approaches are non-empirical, philosophical in nature. For introductions to hermeneutics in its relation to the humanities see: De Boer (1985a), Oudemans & De Jong (1983), and Lubbers (1985). Oudemans (1984) provides a survey of various metatheories of interpretation. For the use of interpretation and hermeneutic approaches in psychology, see Gauld & Shotter (1977), Sass (1988), and Cheshire (1975). The hermeneutic conception of psychoanalysis will be discussed in chapter 5. See also Mooij (1982), Will (1986), and Van Leeuwen (1973). Hermeneutical ideas are further defended in what is called narrative psychology: Sarbin (1986), Carr (1985), Gergen & Gergen (1986); in the literature on metaphors: Danziger (1988), Leary (1988); in so-called qualitative research (Ashworth et al, 1986; Berg & Smith 1985), and in feminist metatheory (M. Gergen 1988).

Chapter 1: Psychology and Philosophy of Science

1. The young discipline of empirical psychology was enchanted by these ideas. Here psychology had found a way to become a respectable member of the traditional sciences, and thus undo its old ties with speculative philosophy. The simpler inductivist-empiricist idea that science proceeds from the objective description of facts to the subsequent creation of theories was immediately embraced by behaviorism. It was used to legitimate the study of the most simple of animal reflexes using the credo: it is facts, facts, facts that we need! One could restrict oneself to uninteresting but objective relations between stimuli and responses because one presupposed that complex behavior would

term 'a-meaningful thinking' in this connection: knowledge was seen as an automatic result of a methodology. (Cf. Koch 1985, Toulmin & Leary 1985). This inductivist belief made behaviorism insensitive to the complexities of human action. Both introspectionism and philosophical anthropology were viewed as irreparably subjective and unscientific. Kurt Danziger (1980) has shown how unjustified this attitude towards various schools of introspectionism has been, and how it involved a falsification of both the history of science and introspectionist theory from the side of behaviorism. For a detailed study of the relation between logical positivism and behaviorism, see Smith (1988).

2. Popper has argued for a method based on the understanding of rational motives for actions in his remarks on what he calls "the logic of the situation". See Popper (1967), Koertge (1975). Yet he has failed to pay attention to the consequences that the adoption of an interpretative methodology based on the "logic of the situation" would have for a falsificationist conception of the social sciences. Popper has been called a hermeneutician by R. Farr (1983), but his article makes it clear, to my mind, that the predicate 'hermeneutician' should be taken with a grain of salt.
3. For an excellent review of the reception Kuhn has received in the social sciences, see Peterson (1981). Bernstein (1983) gives a hermeneutic interpretation of Kuhn's philosophy of science.
4. Kurt Danziger (1985b, 1987, 1989) has pointed out that the results of every psychological experiment are artefacts. Usually the term artefact is used when something has gone wrong, i.e. against the intention of the experimenter, when for instance 'demand-characteristics' play a role. See Hoogstraten (1979). Recognition of the social 'constructed' character of experiments could be very helpful in the often difficult interpretation of the results of experiments. See for instance a reaction to Milgram's well-known obedience experiments: Orne & Holland (1968). Gergen (1978) has given a fundamental critique of the social psychological experiment; cf. Gergen (1982), p. 32 ff. Early insights into the status of experiments were also developed in the Frankfurt School of Critical Psychology by Klaus Holzkamp (1972).

5. A distinction should be made here between branches of psychology that are practically oriented -- social psychology, developmental psychology, clinical psychology -- and forms of experimental psychology dealing with more abstract problems, or even puzzles. My remarks refer to the former, and I doubt whether these practical problems can even be made amenable to empirical-analytical research in a strict sense. This is not to deny the scientific value of social-psychological research; my point is that the explanations given here are structurally similar to common sense explanations, as is more and more recognized within the field: see for instance Furnham et al (1983), Joynson (1974), Jaspars et al (1983), and Billig et al (1988).
6. On the notion of unification in psychology, see Staats et al (1988); various contributions in Stam et al (1987) provide broader perspectives on the context in which unification would have to take place.

Chapter 2: The Early Reception of Psychoanalysis

The Motto to this chapter is to be found in Freud 1925e, p. 217.

1. Cf. chapter 5; Carveth (1984).
   See for a longer Dutch version of this article: Terwee (1987/1988). For critical reactions towards the hermeneutical conception of psychoanalysis, cf. Grünbaum (1984), Strenger (1986).
2. The development of Freud's discoveries is reviewed in length by Schultz (1909; 31 pages), Mittenzwey (1912), hundreds of pages, (comments included), Isserlin (1910, 12 pp.), Kronfeld (1911, 57pp.), and Friedländer (1907b, 13 pages mixed with criticism).
3. Aschaffenburg (Prof. Dr. med., Köln), Hoche, (Prof. Dr. med., Freiburg i.Br.), Friedländer (Privatklinik Hohe Mark, bei Frankfurt a.M.), and Isserlin publish their articles in medical journals; Mittenzwey (München) in the *Zeitschrift für Pathopsychologie*, Friedländer in the *Journal für Psychologie und Neurologie*, and Kronfeld (Dr.med., Assistent der psychiatrischen Klinik der Universität Heidelberg) in the *Archiv für die gesamte Psychologie*.

4. Even Aschaffenburg (1906) is relatively balanced in his judgment (1906, p. 1798), as Jung admitted in his reply (1906, p. 2301). Hoche (1910) is more vigorous and polemical.
5. Freud is respected, his followers generally taken less seriously. Cf. Hoche (1910, p. 1009); Kronfeld (1911, p. 134); Mittenzwey (1912, p. 696). For an impression of the attitude of the psychiatric world to psychoanalysis, see Alt (1907) on a Conference held in Amsterdam, where Jung read a paper.
6. Aschaffenburg (1906, pp. 1796-7); Friedländer (1907b, p. 212); Isserlin (1910, pp. 65, 80); Kronfeld (1911, p. 133).
7. Aschaffenburg's ideas on masturbation leave a more enlightened impression in the modern reader's mind than Freud's (1906, pp. 1793-95).
8. Aschaffenburg (1906, p. 1797); cf. Decker (1981).
9. "Even Freud has to be blamed for this [a lack of taste in the 'game of interpretation'] but he is easily surpassed by some of his adepts. One has only to read what Stekel dares to do in the interpretation of dreams ..." (Isserlin 1910, pp. 74-75).
10. According to Kronfeld, Freud is able to explain everything. "The practice of interpretation itself resembles the guessing of combinations; its standards of truth and its method have never been elaborated in a scientific manner" (1911, p. 243; transl. S.T.). Isserlin is a second author who explicitly deals with Freud's method of interpretation (1910, pp. 66-76). The same critique is given in several reviews of Freud's *Interpretation of Dreams*: see Kimmerle (1986), and *Freud with Hindsight* (Kiell 1988).
11. Mittenzwey (1912, p. 676); Aschaffenburg (1906, p. 1796); Friedländer (1907b, p. 211).
12. Isserlin (1910, p. 79); Kronfeld (1912, p. 132).
13. Mittenzwey (1912, p. 686).
14. The universality of the sexual origins of the neuroses is questioned by Aschaffenburg: he points to therapeutic suggestion which might account for such observations (1906, p. 1797). Jung is careful to reply that the sexual etiology of hysteria is a hypothesis which might be falsified by certain cases in the future

- but has anybody shown us such cases up to now? he asks rhetorically (Jung 1906, p. 2301). Cf. Friedländer (1907a).

15. Decker (1977, 1, p. 321); Decker (1971).
Sulloway (1979, Ch.13).
16. Decker (1977); in chapter 6 she is more cautious.
Decker's research covers the period before 1908.
17. A complete reissue of *Die Fackel* has appeared at the Munich publisher's 2001. Cf. Kraus (n.y.), Schick (1965), Janik & Toulmin (1973).
18. Cf. Freud's letter to Kraus, 12-1-1906 (Freud 1960a).
19. Kraus (1913a), (1913b), Stekel (1913), Wittels (1967); Szasz (1977, pp. 101-151) presents a selection of Kraus' writings on psychoanalysis, psychology, and forensic psychiatry in English translation. I quote his translations. Cf. the *Minutes of the Vienna Psychoanalytic Society* (Nunberg & Federn 1967).
20. In Popper (1963, pp. 33-65). The few remarks in this paper devoted to psychoanalysis (pp. 34-35) have exerted a remarkable influence on discussions on the scientific status of psychoanalysis during the sixties and seventies. Popper does not even try to analyze parts of Freudian theory - perhaps this explains the popularity of his opinions. He wrote: "My problem perhaps first took the simple form, 'What is wrong with Marxism, psychoanalysis, and individual psychology? Why are they so different from physical theories? (1963, p. 34; see also Popper's (1974) Autobiography). Only in 1984, in a Postscript to the *Logic of Scientific Discovery*, Popper delved deeper into the matter when he analyzed the development of Freud's theory of dreams. Here he actually quotes from Freud's work, and this time his conclusions are much more balanced: though Freud is criticized in various ways, he also gets credits for his theorizing. See Popper 1983.
21. Grünbaum (1984, Ch.1, p. 11); see chapter 5, this volume.
22. Freud (1960a), letter to Schnitzler 14-5-1922. Cf. Urban (1978); Schnitzler (1975).
23. For Freud's abandonment of the seduction-theory, cf. Miller (1984), Masson (1985), Krüll (1985), Schusdek (1966), and Ferenczi

(1988).

24. Bolkosky (1986) points to the attention Schnitzler gave to the position of women in Viennese society. See also Gilman (1982).
25. The translations from Schnitzler's (1976) aphorisms are my own (S.T).
26. Cf. chapter 5.
27. Grünbaum (1928) thus gave a first formulation of a hermeneutic conception of psychoanalysis. One could summarize his paper in the following statement: Freud is a crypto-hermeneutician. (Contra F. Sulloway 1979, who maintains that Freud is a crypto-biologist).
28. Wittgenstein's notes on psychoanalysis are not part of a systematic study of Freud. They are scattered in the collection of aphorisms *Culture and Value* (1977) and are written in the period 1931-1951. Rush Rhees has recorded conversations of Freud with Wittgenstein (Barrett 1966, pp. 41-52). He quotes Wittgenstein as saying: 'to learn from Freud you have to be critical; and psychoanalysis generally prevents this' (p. 41). Cf. Terwee (1980).
29. I have changed Peter Winch's translation here.
30. These statements need a more elaborate argumentation. The more liberal attitude may be concluded from modern reaction to Freud's case histories. Analysts from various orientations like Krohn & Krohn (1983), Lewin (1973), Sand (1983), and the contributors to Kanzer & Glenn (1980), feel free to comment on Freud's technical errors, theoretical deficiencies, and arbitrary interpretations. This was not usual, even impossible, in the older literature. Cf. Terwee (1987/88), Graf (1944). So it seems that criticisms from outsiders, once they are formulated in analytic terms and made fruitful for the formulation of alternative models, are sometimes acceptable. There are also examples where hostile criticism from outsiders is consistently disregarded in the analytic community. This happened with Schatzman's (1973) critique of the Schreber Case (Cf. Israels 1980). See Roazen (1975) for more examples. Freud gave a bad example: he couldn't bear criticism from outsiders very well, and usually tried to

explain it away, instead of taking it seriously. Compare, for instance, his reactions to reviews of the *Interpretation of Dreams* in his letters to Fliess (Masson, 1985) with the reviews: Kimmerle (1986), Kiell (1988).

31. Cf. Grünbaum (1928), Carveth (1984), Gergen (1982), Hekman (1984).

Chapter 3: The Case of J. Linschoten's Apostasy

1. Johannes Linschoten was born in Utrecht in 1925, attended secondary school in Bandung, Indonesia (up to 1948 a Dutch colony), and spent three years in a Japanese prison champ during World War II. In 1946 he finished his Gymnasium education in Bilthoven, the Netherlands, and he studied psychology at Utrecht University from 1946-1949. Some biographical information about Linschoten is to be found in Eisenga's (1978) history of Dutch psychology and in Schenk's (1982) study of the Utrecht School of Phenomenology. The information presented above is derived from a biographical sketch in *Idolen van de Psycholoog* (Linschoten 1964). L. Boon (Maastricht University) has conducted interviews with relatives and former colleagues of Linschoten. Nothing has been published so far.
2. On the development of a professional identity in psychology, see Geuter (1984; English translation in preparation), and Ash and Woodward (1987). On the history of the Dutch organization of psychologists see Veldkamp and Van Drunen (1988). For the situation at the Catholic University of Nijmegen: Abma (1983).
3. Schenk (1988) presents details concerning the courses in psychology at Utrecht.
4. On the details of the battle of Gaugamela and the possible tactical significance of Alexander's sleep, see Peter Green's *Alexander of Macedon* (Penguin, 1974). For the importance of psychological research for history see J.D. Hughes, "The Dreams of Alexander the Great", *Journal of Psychohistory* 12 (1984), 168-192.
5. Linschoten never followed Heidegger in his criticism of Husserl (see Th. de Boer, 1978). So he never really accepted the

hermeneutical approach to the humanities as an alternative to the intuition of essences - at least not in his practical psychological work (see Th. de Boer, 1985b). In the essay "The Indispensable Character of Phenomenology" (1963b), Linschoten referred to Wittgenstein's *Blue and Brown Books* and seems to be attracted to the relativistic notion of a language game analysis.

6. As required in the Netherlands, Linschoten's dissertation was published (Linschoten, 1956a).
7. J.H. van den Berg and J. Linschoten, Eds., *Persoon en Wereld* (1953).
8. Gadamer's hermeneutics, inspired by Heidegger's analysis of the structure of time, attributes a historical character to any interpretation (see Gadamer, 1960). On the use of the hermeneutical approach in psychology, see Hekman (1984).
9. Linschoten, 'A Gentle Force', Inaugural Address, University of Utrecht, December 2, 1957 (Linschoten 1957e). In the Netherlands it is customary that a newly-appointed (full) professor assumes his or her responsibilities by giving a public lecture, in which the character of the discipline and the area of specialization are surveyed.
10. As is argued in Linschoten 1963b: a psychological theory has to account for its reductions in everyday language which functions as the paramount metalanguage. The *sensus communis* has its own rights and standing (see Linschoten 1964, p. 64).
11. The phenomenologist Langeveld wrote in a 'In Memoriam' (1964) that Linschoten clearly did not abandon phenomenology, as his essay 'The Indispensable Character of Phenomenology' (Linschoten 1963b) makes clear. A conversation with Linschoten shortly before his death had confirmed this conclusion for Langeveld.
12. H.C.J. Duijker (1965) commented on *Idols* as follows: "It surprises as a 'document humain' because the author distinguishes himself so radically from a doctrine, of which he was considered to be a prominent representative shortly ago ... He may incline to a different extreme just a little bit too much" (p. 632, 644).
13. See chapter 1 on the problems of the growth of knowledge in psychology. On the problems posed by the malleability of human

nature and society to empirical-analytical psychology, see K.J. Gergen (1973, 1982); this volume, chapter 4; and M. Billig (1987).

14. I argue from a hermeneutical conception of psychoanalysis, as defended in chapter 5.
15. For the error contained in Linschoten's argument against Freud's notion of free association, see H.T. Piron (1965). Linschoten's criticism is generally regarded as valid, see Vroon and Draaisma (1985, p. 126); Van Strien (1986, p. 76). Freud's scientism with regard to his own theorizing has been criticized from the early beginnings of psychoanalysis. See Kronfeld (1911) and chapter 2 of this volume.
16. "First order and second order concepts": see Schutz 1954.
17. Immediately after World War II, the number of enrollments in psychology increased rapidly. The Catholic University of Nijmegen counted 33 first matriculations in 1945. Before the war there had never been more than 3 freshmen. The increase had begun during the war. See Abma 1983. With regard to the University of Amsterdam which counted more than 100 freshmen in 1945, see Revesz 1947.
18. Dehue 1986, 1990. On the 'Americanization' of post-war Dutch psychology, see Michon (1986).
19. Strasser 1962, 1970[3].
20. See Kuhn 1962, Ch. 2.
21. See Gergen and Davis (1985), Gergen (1985).
22. Buytendijk writes in his 'In Memoriam' (1964): "Over a period of nine years I have been engaged in countless long-lasting conversations with Linschoten in our intimate small laboratory. During seven years thereafter I have been able to observe from a distance his research in the space of his magnificently designed institute. But although a dialogue had been broken off by this . . . ." (p. 9-11). Buytendijk's words suggest that there had been an estrangement in thinking between the two men in 1957.

Chapter 4: Rhetorical Analysis and Relativism

1. Elsewhere in this volume, different conceptions of rhetoric are discussed: in chapter 1, Michael Billig's (1987) ideas are related

to Kenneth Gergen's. Chapter 7 opens with a short exposition of the "rhetoric of inquiry" developed in the University of Iowa Rhetoric Seminar (Nelson, Megill & McCloskey 1987). The three rhetorical approaches thus indicated share a number of features. In each case, we may note (a) an interest in non-rational factors in science; (b) that the traditional dichotomy between rationality and non-rational elements is questioned; (c) that absolute foundations for knowledge are rejected; (d) a fascination with persuasive strategies used by and inherent in science; and (e) recognition of the tropological function of language and scientific discourse, which constitute the world of objects.

The idea that scientific discourse constitutes the world is a more radical formulation of the insight that facts are theory-laden. If this is true (i.e. if it is a good, fruitful idea, which can be supported by arguments) it still does not imply that we are free to invent theories in complete disregard of the actual world. That is my point in chapter 4.

This is not to say that the lifeworld, or common sense, or any form of life, is able to present us a clear and unambiguous conception of truth. There is never a highest authority, as Michael Billig has illustrated very neatly with a Rabbinical Story: "A heavenly voice was heard by all to say: 'Why do you quarrel with Rabbi Eliezer, who is always right in his decisions?' That was not the end of the matter. Rabbi Joshua answered the heavenly voice back by quoting from the Bible: 'The Law is not in the heavens.' The Law, indeed all laws, lay now in earthly discussions" (Billig 1987, p. 30).

However, many theses and opinions, as well as theories, are extremely difficult to argue for because all sorts of certainties are shared by most members of a certain form of life. So I do not claim against Kenneth Gergen that truth is unambiguous because it rests on truth contained in our form of life. Rather, my argument is that we may still sensibly use the concept of truth (with all the ambiguities associated with it) thanks to the certainties of our form of life.

Chapter 5: The Hermeneutical Conception of Psychoanalysis

1. Reading Popper's (1963) arguments against depth-psychological pseudo-reasoning, one gains the impression that this criticism is not primarily leveled against Freud's work or theories (not a single quotation or theoretical statement is discussed) but against a peculiar psychological way of thinking which flourished in Vienna in the first decades of this century. The eminent Viennese satirist Karl Kraus (1913a, b) repeatedly criticized this way of thinking in his journal *Die Fackel*, on the grounds that it embodied a set of rhetorical power-tactics to immunize the psychologist and make his victims helpless. Kraus was particularly enraged by 'psychoanalyses' of helpless victims: artists whose work was reduced to neurotic products and criminals within forensic psychiatry. Thomas Szasz (1977) has called attention to Kraus's influence on Popper. Indeed it seems plausible that the criterion of falsifiability was first developed as a moral weapon against totalitarian ideas present in Marxism and certain versions of psychoanalysis.
2. As far as known, this article has never been translated into English. All quotations from Grünbaum (1928) have been translated from the German by the author.
3. See for the concepts of language game and rule following Wittgenstein's *Philosophical Investigations* (1953). The difference between a rule and a mere regularity is also pointed out clearly by Ryle (1949), chapter 2, Searle (1969), and Duintjer (1977), who provides a list of characteristics of rule following. Peters (1958) has stressed the importance of the rule following purposive pattern into which we fit our common sense explanations. He analyzes Freud's theory with the help of these concepts. Compare Toulmin (1954) and Taylor (1964). In formulating my ideas on the logic of explanation I have profited from comments made by W.F. van Leeuwen on an earlier draft.
4. As T.S. Kuhn puts it, "Surely the plausibility of a historical narrative does not depend upon the power of a few scattered and doubtful laws. An ability to predict the future is not part of the historian's arsenal. (...) The historian at work is governed

by rules that may not be violated. There may be no empty spaces (or) discontinuities ... Nothing in the narrative may, for example, do violence to the facts ... Such rules however, only limit but do not determine the outcome ..." (Kuhn 1977, pp. 16-17).

5. We must exclude representatives of an objectivistic hermeneutics, like E.D. Hirsch (1967), from this generalization.
6. Gergen (1982) and Runyan (1982) have argued for the acceptance of an interpretative approach within academic psychology. See also the Introduction, note 1, in this volume.
7. For an example of this condescending attitude towards interpretations in psychology, see A.D. de Groot (1961), pp. 325-343. More recently, it has been argued by psychologists that there are subjects which cannot be approached objectively in a sensible way, such as quality-judgments (Hofstee 1985b). After a century of psychology as a science (Koch & Leary 1985), the time has come to evaluate the results of objective empirical-analytical methods. Defenders of 'hard' objective methods in the humanities have many sound arguments at their disposal, but they have to admit that their methods are not a guarantee against fraud (Broad & Wade 1985), that emotional factors still play a role in research (Devereux 1967), that computer programs and statistical techniques are frequently used in an irrational way (Leeuw & Mooijaart 1987, Bakan 1970, Tholey 1982). In the light of all this, the ideal of objectivity and the denunciation of subjectivity in hermeneutical approaches reminds one of the opposition between purity and pollution so interestingly described by anthropologist Mary Douglas (1966).

Chapter 6: The Case of Ergonomics

1. For introductions to the psychological study of decision-making, see Vlek & Wagenaar (1979) and Vlek (1987). For various approaches to the study of risk-taking and accidents, see Wagenaar (1986b, 1987c), Hofstee (1987), Wagenaar & Keren (1986), and Douglas (1985).
2. Personal communication by A.D. de Groot, 3-2-1988. The question is a free translation of various comments made by De Groot on

an earlier paper I wrote on hermeneutics.

3. Rob Roe, Over welke mensen gaat psychologie eigenlijk? *De Psycholoog* 24 (1989), 67-73. Reactions and an answer by Roe: pp. 74-79 & 135-139. Both the diagnosis of psychology's present knowledge and the remedies Roe proposes show a similarity with my line of argument, though they are made from a very different perspective. Roe does not use the term hermeneutics.

Chapter 7: A Rhetorical Approach to Dream Theories and Dreams

1. This point is also made by Bert O. States in *The Rhetoric of Dreams* (1988), a book which came to my attention after writing this chapter. States argues from the same assumption as Rycroft - rehabilitation of dream processes as an independent, adaptive form of the imagination - but notes that "Rycroft has thrown out the unconscious in one form only to admit it in another ..." (p. 27). States finds the notion of self-to-self communication problematic. I agree with him that we should think of this kind of communication metaphorically, as a 'dialectical habit of thought', also manifested in many daily situations, as Michael Billig has argued. Psychologists are often tempted to take the clinical situation, where a patient communicates dreams to a therapist, as their point of departure. See Kuiken (1986).
2. Hobson (1988) is quite clear about his dislike of ambiguousness and his preference of clear-cut empirical (or empiricist) methods. For instance, in connection to Freud's 'anecdotes' in *The Interpretation of Dreams* he observes that they "do not qualify even as observations; ... their interpretation more closely resembles speculative literary criticism than it does scientific reasoning" (1988, p.57).
3. For the literature on chaos, see Crutchfield et al (1986), Tritton (1986), Pool (1989), and Davies (1989). Also relevant in connection to the adequate mapping of reality in models is Zeeman's (1976) Catastrophe Theory.
4. States (1988) views dreams as experiences that resemble, but are differently organized than language. The production of images in dreams has parallels with art-making, though it is not meant to

reach an audience. The same talent for image-making is involved. States starts from a different vantage point than most neurophysiologists and cognitive psychologists when he wonders how the dream manages to remain so *orderly* in its operations. "In sleep, one would think that a mind free of the involvements of putting one foot before another and reduced to a helpless receptor of sensation would run away with itself and produce a chaos of images, or nothing at all. ... In fact, most dreams are conservative when compared with the distortions we find in poetry and art" (p. 83).

5. A hypothesis comparable with that of Crick & Mitchison has been advanced by Christopher Evans in *Landscapes of the Night* (1983). He regards the dreaming brain as a computer which goes off line to update its library of programs, and sort and scan material.
6. One of the first analysts who came to doubt the necessity of distance was Sandor Ferenczi: see his interesting *Clinical Diary* (1988). In his practical work, Freud himself was not strictly adhering to his metaphor of the mirror. He found it useful to stress the importance of objectivity, while at the same time being very much personally involved. The same is true for his *Interpretation of Dreams*: though Freud claims that interpreting a dream is like solving a puzzle, which implies that there is only one solution, his subjectivity cannot be denied. David Willbern (1979) has aptly spoken of Freud's "inter-penetration" of dreams. See the excellent article by Jim Swan (1974) on the relation between Freud's personal life and his theories. Schorske (1980) has drawn attention to the political contents of Freud's dreams and wishes. A present-day example of orthodox psychoanalytic understanding of the dream is Sloane (1979). For surveys of current approaches to dream interpretation, see Jones (1978), Hudson (1985), and Fosshage & Loew (1978). Finally, for an attempt to interpret dreams objectively, see Foulkes' (1978) scoring system. In a more recent book, Foulkes (1985) seems to have lost confidence in his system.

BIBLIOGRAPHY

Abel, Th. (1975) 'Verstehen I and Verstehen II'. *Theory and Decision* 6, 99-102.

Abma, Ruud (1983) *Methodisch zonder confessie. Uit de geschiedenis van de Nijmeegse psychologie.* Nijmegen: Psychologisch Laboratorium, KUN.

Alt, Konrad (1907) Bericht: Internationaler Kongress für Psychiatrie, Neurologie, Psychologie und Kranksinnigen-Verpflegung, Amsterdam, 2-7 Sept. 1907. *Monatsschrift für Psychiatrie und Neurologie* 22, 562-572.

Ankersmit, F.R. (1984) *Denken over geschiedenis.* Baarn: Ambo.

Aristotle (1926) *Nichomachean Ethics* (NE). Translation H. Rackham. Loeb Classical Library. London: Heinemann, 1975.

Aschaffenburg, G. (1906) Die Beziehungen des sexuellen Lebens zur Entstehung von Nerven- und Geisteskrankheiten. *Münchener Medizinische Wochenschrift* 53, 1793-1798.

Ash, Mitchell G. & Woodward, William R. (eds.) (1987) *Psychology in Twentieth Century Thought and Society.* Cambridge: Cambridge University Press.

Ashworth, P.D., Giorgi, A., & De Koning, A.J.J. (eds.) (1986) *Qualitative Research in Psychology.* Pittsburgh: Duquesne University Press.

Bakan, David (1970) The Test of Significance in Psychological Research. In: Denton E. Morrison & Ramon E. Henkel (eds.), *The Significance Test Controversy.* London: Butterworths, 231-251.

Baker, Wm. J., Mos, L.P., Rappard, H.V. & Stam, H.J. (eds.) (1988) *Recent Trends in Theoretical Psychology.* New York: Springer-Verlag.

Barrett, Cyril (ed.) (1966) *Wittgenstein: Lectures and Conversations on Aesthetics, Psychology and Religious Belief.* Oxford: Basil Blackwell.

Bartels, M. (1979) Ist der Traum eine Wunscherfüllung? *Psyche* 33, 97-131.

Beijk, J. & Roskam, Edw. E. (red.) (1977) De crisis in de psychologie. Themanummer van het *Nederlands tijdschrift voor de psychologie en haar grensgebieden* 32, 171-259.

Berg, D.N. & Smith, K.K. (eds.) (1985) *Exploring Clinical Methods for Social Research.* Beverly Hills: Sage Publications.

Bernfeld, S. (1962), On Psychoanalytic Training. *Psychoanalytical Quarterly* 31, pp. 453-482

Bernheimer, C., & Kahane, C. (eds.) (1985) *In Dora's Case. Freud-Hysteria-Feminism.* New York: Columbia University Press.

Bernstein, R.J. (1983) *Beyond Objectivism and Relativism: Science, Hermeneutics and Praxis.* Philadelphia: Basil Blackwell.

Billig, Michael (1987) *Arguing and thinking. A rhetorical approach to social psychology.* Cambridge: Cambridge University Press.

Billig, Michael et al (1988). *Ideological Dilemmas.* A Social Psychology of Everyday Thinking. London: Sage.

Blight, J.G. (1981) Must psychoanalysis retreat to hermeneutics? *Psychoanalysis and Contemporary Thought* 4, 147-205.

Boer, Th. de & Köbben, A. (red.) (1974) *Waarden en wetenschap.* Bilthoven: Ambo.

Boer, Th. de (1978) Heideggers kritiek op Husserl. *Tijdschrift voor Filosofie* 40, 202-225 & 452-501.

Boer, Th. de (1983a) *Foundations of a Critical Psychology* (translated by T. Plantinga). Pittsburgh: Duquesne University Press.

Boer, Th. de (1983b) De vraag naar de psychologie: Kritik der unreinen Vernunft. In: Drenth, P.J.D., et al. *Psychologie in Nederland. Enkele ontwikkelingen in 1982.* Lisse: Swets & Zeitlinger, 1-24.

Boer, Th. de (1985a) Zelfkennis en wetenschap van de mens. In: M.G.M. van den Dungen et al (eds.) *Tussen ideologie en opvoedingswerkelijkheid.* Amsterdam: Orthopedagogisch Instituut, 29-67.

Boer, Th. de (1985b) Van wezensschouw naar hermeneuse. Over de methode van de filosofie. *Algemeen Nederlands Tijdschrift voor Wijsbegeerte* 77, 36-59.

Boer, Th. de, et al (red.) (1988) *Hermeneutiek - Filosofische grondslagen van mens- en cultuurwetenschappen.* Meppel: Boom.

Boheemen, Christine van (1987) *The Novel as Family Romance. Language, Gender, and Authority from Fielding to Joyce.* Ithaca: Cornell University Press.

Bolkosky, S. (1986) Arthur Schnitzler and the Fate of Mothers in Vienna. *Psychoanalytic Review* 73, 1-15.

Borst, C.V. (1970) (ed). *The Mind/Brain Identity Theory.* London: The Macmillan Press.

Brandt, L.W. (1982) *Psychologists Caught. A Psycho-Logic of Psychology.* Toronto: University of Toronto Press.

Broad, W. & Wade, N. (1985) *Betrayers of the Truth. Fraud and Deceit in Science.* Oxford: Oxford University Press.

Buytendijk, F.J.J. (1964) In Memoriam Johannes Linschoten. *Jaarboek der Rijksuniversiteit Utrecht 1963-1964*, 9-11.

Carr, David (1985) Life and the Narrator's Art. In: H.J. Silverman & D. Ihde (eds.) *Hermeneutics & Deconstruction.* Stony Brook: State University of New York Press, 108-121.

Cartwright, D. (1973) Determinants of scientific progress: The case of the Risky Shift. *American Psychologist* 28, 222-231.

Carveth, D.L. (1984) The Analyst's Metaphors: A Deconstructionist Perspective. *Psychoanalysis and Contemporary Thought* 7, 491-560.

Cheshire, N.M. (1975) *The Nature of Psycho-dynamic Interpretation.* New York: John Wiley & Sons.

Crick, F. & Mitchison, G. (1983). The Function of Dream Sleep. *Nature* 304, 111-114.

Crick, Francis, Mitchison, Greame (1986). REM Sleep and Neural Nets. *The Journal of Mind and Behavior* 7, 229-249.

Crombag, H.F.M., L.J.Th. van der Kamp, & C.A.J. Vlek (red.) (1987) *De psychologie voorbij. Ontwikkelingen rond model, metriek en methode in de gedragswetenschappen.* Lisse: Swets & Zeitlinger.

Crutchfield, J.P. et al (1986) Chaos. *Scientific American* 255/6, 38-49.

Danziger, K. (1980) The History of Introspection Reconsidered. *J. Hist. Behav. Sc.* 16, 241-262.

Danziger, Kurt (1985a) The Methodological Imperative in Psychology. *Phil. Soc. Sci.* 15, 1-13.

Danziger, Kurt (1985b) The origin of the psychological experiment as a social institution. *American Psychologist* 40, 133-140.

Psychological Discourse. In: Leary, D.E. (ed.), *Metaphors in the History of Psychology.*

Danziger, Kurt (1989) Psychologische experimenten als sociale praktijk: historische overwegingen. *Kennis en Methode* 13, 146-158.

Davies, Paul (1987) The Creative Cosmos. *New Scientist* 116, no. 1591, 41-44.

Decker, H.S. (1971) The medical reception of psychoanalysis in Germany, 1894-1907: Three brief studies. *Bulletin of the History of Medicine* 45, 461-81.

Decker, H.S. (1977) Freud in Germany. Revolution and Reaction in Science, 1893-1907. *Psychological Issues* 11/4, monograph 41.

Decker, H.S. (1981) Freud and Dora: Constraints on medical progress. *Journal of Social History* 14, 445-464.

Dehue, T. (1986) Handschrift en karakter. De Amerikaanse wending in de Nederlandse psychodiagnostiek. In: Koenis & Plantenga (eds.), *Amerika en de sociale wetenschappen in Nederland*, 78-112.

Dehue, T. (1990) *De regels van het vak: de Nederlandse psychologie en haar methodologie.* Amsterdam: van Gennep

Derksen, A.A. (1980) *Rationaliteit en wetenschap.* Assen: Van Gorcum.

Devereux, George (1967) *From Anxiety to Method in the Behavioral Sciences.* The Hague: Mouton.

Douglas, Mary (1966) *Purity and Danger. An Analysis of the Concepts of Pollution and Taboo.* London: Routledge & Kegan Paul (1979).

Douglas, Mary (1985) *Risk Acceptability According to the Social Sciences.* New York: Russell Sage Foundation.

Dray, William (1957) *Laws and Explanation in History.* Oxford: At the Clarendon Press.

Duhem, P. (1954) *The Aim and Structure of Physical Theory*, transl. by P.P. Wiener. Princeton: Princeton University Press.

Duintjer, O.D. (1970) Moderne wetenschap en waardevrijheid. *ANTW* 62, 22-44. (Also in: Th. de Boer & A. Köbben (red.), *Waarden en wetenschap.* Baarn: Ambo (1974), 20-45).

Duintjer, O.D. (1977) *Rondom regels.* Meppel: Boom.

Duijker, H.C.J. (1965) Idolen uit machines. *Nederlands Tijdschrift voor de Psychologie* 20, 623-644.

Eagle, M.N. (1980) A Critical Examination of Motivational Explanation in Psychoanalysis. *Psychoanalysis and Contemporary Thought* 3, 329-380.

Edmunds, L. (1985) Freud and the father. Oedipus-complex and Oedipus-myth. *Psychoanalysis and Contemporary Thought* 8, 87-103.

Ehebald, Ulrich (1980) Überlegungen zur Einschätzung des manifesten Traumes. In: Frijling-Schreuder, B. et al (eds.): *Psychoanalytici aan het woord*, Deventer: Van Loghum Slaterus, pp 37-54.

Einhorn, H.J. & Hogarth, R.M. (1987) Decision making: going forward in reverse. *Harvard Business Review* 65, 66-70.

Eisenga, L.K.A. (1978) *Geschiedenis van de Nederlandse psychologie.* Deventer: Van Loghum Slaterus.

Erdelyi, M.H. (1985) *Psychoanalysis: Freud's Cognitive Psychology.* New York: W.H. Freeman.

Evans, Christopher (1983) *Landscapes of the Night.* New York: The Viking Press.

Farr, James (1983) Popper's Hermeneutics. *Philosophy of the Social Sciences* 13, 157-176.

Ferenczi, Sandor (1988) *Clinical Diary.* Cambridge, Mass.: Harvard University Press.

Feyerabend, Paul (1970) Consolations for the Specialist. In: Lakatos, I. & Musgrave, A. (eds.) *Criticism and the Growth of Knowledge.* Cambridge: Cambridge University Press, 197-230.

Fischhoff, Baruch & Beyth-Marom, Ruth (1983) Hypothesis Evaluation from a Bayesian Perspective. *Psychological Review* 90, 239-260.

Forrester, John (1986) Essay Review of A. Grünbaum, The Foundations of Psychoanalysis. *Isis* 77, 670-674.

Fosshage, J.L. & Loew, C.A. (eds.) (1978) *Dream Interpretation - A Comparative Study.* New York: Spectrum Publications.

Fosshage, James L. (1983). The Psychological Function of Dreams: A Revised Psychoanalytic Perspective. *Psychoanalysis and Contemporary Thought* 6, 641-669.

Foulkes, David (1978). *A Grammar of Dreams.* Hassocks: Harvester Press.

Foulkes, David (1985). *Dreaming: A Cognitive-psychological Analysis.* London: Erlbaum.

Frank, M. (1984) Die Grenzen der Beherrschbarkeit der Sprache. In: P. Forget (ed.), *Text und Interpretation*. München: Wilhelm Fink Verlag, 181-213.

French, T.M. & Fromm, E. (1964) *Dream Interpretation. A New Approach*. New York: Basic Books.

Freud, S. *Standard Edition of the Complete Psychological Works of Sigmund Freud*. London: The Hogarth Press, 1953-1974.

Freud, S. (1900a) The Interpretation of Dreams. *Standard Edition*, Vol. 4-5.

Freud, S. (1901b) The Psychopathology of Everyday Life. *Standard Edition* 6: 1-279.

Freud, S. (1912e) Recommendations to Physicians Practising Psycho-Analysis. *Standard Edition* 12: 109-120.

Freud, S. (1925e) The resistances to Psycho-Analysis. *Standard Edition* 19: 211-222.

Freud, S. (1926e) The Question of Lay-Analysis. *Standard Edition* 20: 177-250.

Freud, S. (1937a) Analysis Terminable and Interminable. *Standard Edition* 23: 209-253.

Freud, S. (1937b) Constructions in Analysis. *Standard Edition* 23: 255-269.

Freud, S. (1960a) *Briefe 1873-1939*. Frankfurt: S. Fischer Verlag.

Friedländer, A. (1907a) Über Hysterie und die Freudsche psychoanalytische Behandlung derselben. *Monatsschrift für Psychiatrie und Neurologie* 22, 45-54.

Friedländer, A. (1907b) Sammelreferat. S. Freuds neuere Abhandlungen zur Neurosenfrage. *Journal für Psychologie und Neurologie* 10, 201-213.

Fromm, Erich (1951) *The Forgotten Language. An Introduction to the Understanding of Dreams, Fairy Tales and Myths*. New York: Rinehart & Co.

Furnham, A., Jaspars, J. & Fincham, F. (1983) Professional and Naive Psychology: Two Approaches to the Explanation of Social Behaviour. In: J. Jaspars et al.(eds.), *Attribution Theory and Research*. London: Academic Press, pp. 315-340.

Gackenbach, J. & La Berge, S.P. (eds) (1988) *Conscious Mind, Sleeping Brain*. New York: Plenum Press.

Gadamer, Hans-Georg (1960) *Wahrheit und Methode. Grundzüge einer philosophischen Hermeneutik.* Tübingen: J.C.B. Mohr (1972^3). Translation: *Truth and Method.* New York: Seabury Press (1979^2).

Gauld, A. & Shotter, J. (1977) *Human Action and its Psychological Investigation.* London: Routledge & Kegan Paul 1980.

Gergen, Kenneth J. (1973) Social Psychology as History. *J. Pers. Soc. Psychol.* 26, 309-320.

Gergen, K.J. (1978) Experimentation in Social Psychology: A Reappraisal. *European J. Soc. Psychol.* 8, 507-527.

Gergen, K.J. (1980) Towards Intellectual Audacity in Social Psychology. In: Gilmour, R. & Duck, S. (eds.), *The Development of Social Psychology.* London: Academic Press, pp. 239-270.

Gergen, Kenneth J. (1982) *Toward Transformation in Social Knowledge.* New York: Springer.

Gergen, K.J. (1985a) Social Constructionist Inquiry: Context and Implications. In: K.J. Gergen & K.E. Davis 1985, *The social construction of the person.* New York: Springer, 3-18.

Gergen, K.J. (1985b) The Social Constructionist Movement in Modern Psychology. *American Psychologist*, 40, 266-275.

Gergen, K.J. (1986) Interpreting Texts of Nature and Culture: A Reply to Jahoda. *Eur. J. Soc. Psych.* 16, 31-37.

Gergen, K.J. (1988) If Persons are Texts. In: S.B. Messer, L.A. Sass & R.L. Woolfolk (eds.) *Hermeneutics and Psychological Theory.* New Brunswick, N.J.: Rutgers University Press, pp. 28-51.

Gergen, K.J. & Davis, K.E. (eds.) (1985) *The Social Construction of the Person.* New York: Springer.

Gergen, K.J., Hepburn, A. & Comer Fisher, D. (1986) Hermeneutics of personality description. *J. Pers. Soc. Psychol.* 50, 1261-70.

Gergen, Kenneth J. & Gergen, Mary M. (1986) Narrative Form and the Construction of Psychological Science. In: Th. Sarbin (ed.), *Narrative Psychology.* New York: Praeger, 22-44.

Gergen, Mary (1988) Toward a Feminist Metatheory and Methodology in the Social Sciences. In: Gergen, M.M. (ed.), *Feminist Thought and the Structure of Knowledge.* New York: New York U.P.,87-

Geuter, Ulfried (1984) *Die Professionalisierung der deutschen Psychologie im Nationalsozialismus.* Frankfurt: Suhrkamp.

Gilman, S. (1982) Das männliche Stereotyp von der weiblichen Sexualität im Wiener Fin de Siècle. *Jahrbuch der Psychoanalyse* 14, 236-263.

Giorgi, Amedeo (1982) Issues relating to the meaning of psychology as a science. In: *Contemporary Philosophy. A New Survey*, Vol. 2. The Hague: Martinus Nijhoff, 317-342.

Graf, Max (1942) Reminiscences of Professor Sigmund Freud. *Ps. An. Quart.* 2, 465-477.

Green, Peter (1974) *Alexander of Macedon.* Harmondsworth: Penguin.

Groot, A.D. de (1947) Een experimenteel-statistische toetsing van karakterologische (grafologische) rapporten. *Ned. Tijdschrift voor de Psychologie* 2, 380-473.

Groot, A.D. de (1961) *Methodologie.* 's Gravenhage: Mouton, 1970[3]. (Translation: *Methodology. Foundations of Inference and Research in the Behavioral Sciences.* The Hague: Mouton, 1969. Quotations refer to the Dutch edition).

Groot, A.D. de (1990) Unifying Psychology: Its Preconditions. In: W. Baker et al (eds.). *Recent Trends in Theoretical Psychology, Vol. II. New York: Springer.*

Grünbaum, A.A. (1915) Zur Psychologie der Träume. *Psychiatrische en Neurologische Bladen* 19, 409-425.

Grünbaum, A.A. (1928) Die Idee der Psychoanalyse und die Erkenntnistheorie. In: H. Prinzhorn (Hsg) *Krisis der Psychoanalyse, Band I*, 196-211. Leipzig: Der Neue Geist Verlag.

Grünbaum, Adolf (1984) *The Foundations of Psychoanalysis. A Philosophical Critique.* Berkeley: Univ. of California Press.

Habermas, Jürgen (1968) *Knowledge and Human Interests.* London: Heinemann 1978. (Includes Appendix)

Hekman, Susan (1984) Action as a Text: Gadamer's Hermeneutics and the Social Scientific Analysis of Action. *J. for the Theory of Social Behaviour* 14, 333-354.

Hempel, C.G. (1965) *Aspects of Scientific Explanation.* New York: The Free Press.

Hirsch, E.D. (1967) *Validity in Interpretation.* New Haven: Yale University Press.

Hobson, J. & McCarley, R. (1977) The brain as a dream state generator: An activation-synthesis hypothesis of the dream process. *American Journal of Psychiatry* 134, 1335-48.

Hobson, J.A., Lydic, R. & Baghdoyan, H.A. (1986). Evolving concepts of sleep cycle generation: From brain centers to neuronal populations. *The Behavioral and Brain Sciences* 9, 371-448.

Hobson, J. Allan (1988) *The Dreaming Brain.* New York: Basic Books.

Hoche, A. (1910) Eine psychische Epidemie under Aertzten. *Medizinische Klinik* 26, 1007-1010.

Hofstee, W.K.B. (1980) *De empirische discussie. Theorie van het sociaal-wetenschappelijk onderzoek.* Meppel: Boom.

Hofstee, W.K.B. (1985a) Bespreking van G. de Vries, 'De ontwikkeling van wetenschap'. *Nederlands Tijdschrift voor de Psychologie* 40, 301-304.

Hofstee, W.K.B. (1985b) Liever klinisch? Grenzen aan het objectiviteitsbeginsel bij beoordeling en selectie. *Nederlands Tijdschrift voor de Psychologie* 40, 459-473.

Hofstee, W.K.B. (1987) Wiens risico's lopen wij? *Nederlands Tijdschrift voor de Psychologie* 42, 47-53.

Holzkamp, Klaus (1972) *Kritische Psychologie.* Frankfurt: Fischer.

Hoogstraten, J. (1979) *De machteloze onderzoeker.* Meppel: Boom.

Hudson, Liam (1985). *Night Life. The Interpretation of Dreams.* London: Weidenfeld & Nicolson.

Hughes, J.D. (1984) The Dreams of Alexander the Great. *Journal of Psychohistory* 12, 168-192.

Husserl, Edmund (1935) *Die Krisis der europäischen Wissenschaften und die transzendentale Phänomenologie.* Husserliana, Band VI, 1954. The Hague: Martinus Nijhoff.

Israels, Han (1980) *Schreber. Father and Son.* New York: Madison.

Isserlin, Max (1910) Die psychoanalytische Methode Freuds. *Zeitschrift für die gesamte Neurologie und Psychiatrie*, 52-80.

Jahoda, Gustav (1986) Nature, culture and social psychology. *Eur. J. of Soc. Psychol.* 16, 17-30.

Janik, A. and Toulmin, S. (1973) *Wittgenstein's Vienna.* New York: Simon & Schuster.

Jones, E. (1955) *Sigmund Freud, Life and Work. Volume II.* London: The Hogarth Press, 1974.

Jones, Richard M. (1978). *The New Psychology of Dreaming*. Harmondsworth: Penguin books.

Joynson, R.B. (1974) *Psychology and Common Sense*. London: Routledge & Kegan Paul.

Jung, C.G. (1906) Die Hysterielehre Freuds. *Münchener medizinische Wochenschrift* 53, 2301-02.

Jung, C.G. (1934/1974) *Dreams*. Princeton: Princeton University Press.

Jung, C.G. (1984) *Dream Analysis. Notes of the Seminar Given in 1928-1930*. Princeton: Princeton University Press.

Kanzer, Mark & Glenn, Jules (eds.) (1980) *Freud and His Patients*. New York: Jason Aronson.

Keats, John (1978). Letter to G. & T. Keats, December 1817. In: H. Bloom & L. Trilling (eds.), *The Oxford Anthology of English Literature*, Vol. II, p. 768. Oxford: Oxford University Press.

Kiell, Norman (1988) *Freud Without Hindsight. Reviews of His Work (1893-1939)*. Madison: International Universities Press.

Kimmerle, Gerd (1986) (ed.) *Freuds Traumdeutung. Frühe Rezensionen 1899-1903*. Tübingen: Edition Diskord.

Koch, Sigmund (1981) The Nature and Limits of Psychological Knowledge. *American Psychologist* 36, 257-269.

Koch, Sigmund (1985) Afterword. In: Koch, S. & Leary, D. (eds.), *A Century of Psychology as a Science. New York: McGraw-Hill, pp. 928-950.*

Koele, Pieter (1979) Afscheid van de nulhypothese. Statistische consequenties van een kritisch rationalistische wetenschapsopvatting. *Kennis en Methode* 3, 446-458.

Koenis, S. & Plantenga, J. (eds.) (1986) *Amerika en de sociale wetenschappen in Nederland*. Utrecht: Grafiet.

Koertge, Noretta (1975) Popper's Metaphysical Research Program for the Human Sciences. *Inquiry* 18, 437-462.

Kouwer, B.J. & Linschoten, J. (1951) *Inleiding tot de psychologie*. Assen: Born.

Kraus, Karl (n.y.) *Ausgewählte Werke Band I: Grimassen, 1902-1914*. München: Kösel Verlag.

Kraus, K. (1913a) Aphorismen über die Psychoanalyse. *Die Fackel*, nr. 376/377.

Kraus, K. (1913b) Unbefügte Psychologie. In: *Grimassen, Ausgewählte Werke I.*

Krohn, Alan & Krohn, Janis (1982) The Nature of the Oedipus Complex in the Dora Case. *J. of the Amer. Psychoanal. Ass.* 30, 555-578.

Kronfeld, Arthur (1911) Über die psychologischen Theorien Freuds und verwandte Anschauungen. Systematik und kritische Erörterung. *Archiv für die gesamte Psychologie* 22, 130-248.

Krüll, M. (1985) *Freud and His Father.* New York: Norton.

Kuhn, T.S. (1962) *The Structure of Scientific Revolutions.* Second edition, enlarged with a Postscript (1970). Chicago: University of Chicago Press.

Kuhn, Thomas S. (1977) *The Essential Tension.* Chicago: University of Chicago Press.

Kuiken, Don (1986) Dreams and Self-Knowledge. In: J. Gackenbach (ed.), *Sleep and Dreams: A Sourcebook.* New York: Garland, 225-250.

Kuper, Adam (1979) A Structural Approach to Dreams. *Man (N.S.)* 14, 645-662.

Kuper, Adam (1986) Structural Anthropology and the Psychology of Dreams. *The Journal of Mind and Behavior* 7, 333-344.

Lakatos, Imre (1970) Falsification and the Methodology of Scientific Research Programmes. In: Lakatos & Musgrave (eds.) *Criticism and the Growth of Knowledge.* Cambridge: Cambridge University Press.

Lakatos, I. & Musgrave, A. (eds.) (1970) *Criticism and the Growth of Knowledge.* Cambridge: Cambridge University Press, 91-196.

Langeveld, M.J. (1964) In Memoriam Prof.dr. J. Linschoten. *Nederlands Tijdschrift voor de Psychologie* 19, 101-103.

Leary, David E. (ed.) (1988) *Metaphors in the History of Psychology.*

Leeuw, J. de & A. Mooijaart (1987) Multivariate analyse van lineaire structurele modellen. In: Crombag e.a., *De psychologie voorbij*, 167-182.

Leeuwen, W.F. van (1973) Het psychoanalytisch minimum. In: A.P. Cassee et al (eds), *Klinische psychologie in Nederland.* Deventer: Van Loghum Slaterus, 56-79.

Lewin, K.K. (1973) Dora Revisited. *The Psychoanalytic Review*, 60, 519-532.

Linschoten, J. (1950) Logische en phenomenologische analyse der bewegingsverschijnselen. *Tijdschrift voor Philosophie* 12, 668-728.
Linschoten, J. (1951a) Over de humor. *Tijdschrift voor Philosophie* 13, 603-666.
Linschoten, J. (1952) Over het inslapen. *Tijdschrift voor Philosophie* 14, 207-264.
Linschoten, J. (1953a) Aspecten van de sexuele incarnatie. In: Berg, J.H. van den & Linschoten, J. (red.) *Persoon en wereld. Bijdragen tot de phaenomenologische Psychologie.* Utrecht: Bijleveld, 74-126.
Linschoten, J. (1953b) Nawoord. In: Van den Berg, J.H. & Linschoten, J. (red.) *Persoon en wereld. Bijdragen tot de phaenomenologische Psychologie.* Utrecht: Bijleveld, 244-253.
Linschoten, J. (1956a) *Strukturanalyse der binokularen Tiefwahrnehmung.* (academisch proefschrift) Groningen: Wolters.
Linschoten, J. (1956b) *Psychische moeilijkheden.* Haarlem: De Toorts.
Linschoten, J. (1957) 'L'esprit scientifique doit se former contre la nature.' Critische beschouwingen over de metabletica. *Kultuurleven* 24, 498-510.
Linschoten, J. (1957e) A gentle force. Beschouwingen over het associatiebegrip. (Inaugurele rede Utrecht) Groningen: Wolters.
Linschoten, J. (1959c) *Op weg naar een fenomenologische psychologie.* Utrecht: Bijleveld.
Linschoten, J. (1963b) Die Unumgänglichkeit der Phänomenologie. *Jahrbuch für Psychologie, Psychotherapie und medizinische Anthropologie* 10, 177-185.
Linschoten, J. (1964) *Idolen van de psycholoog.* Utrecht: Bijleveld.
Linschoten, Hans (1968) *On the way toward a Phenomenological Psychology: The Psychology of William James.* Edited by Amedeo Giorgi. Pittsburgh: Duquesne University Press. (Translation of: 1959c)
Losee, John (1979) *A Historical Introduction to the Philosophy of Science* (Second Edition). Oxford: Oxford University Press.
Lubbers, R. (red.) (1985) *Hermeneutische diagnostiek en probleemoplossing.* Nijmegen: Dekker & V.d. Vegt.
MacNamara, J., Govitrikar, V.P. & Doan, B. (1988) Actions, laws, and scientific psychology. *Cognition* 29, 1-27.

Masson, J.J. (1985) (ed.). *The Complete Letters of Sigmund Freud to Wilhelm Fliess*. Cambridge, Mass.: The Belknap Press.

McCloskey, Donald N. (1983). The Rhetoric of Economics. *Journal of Economic Literature* 21, 481-517.

Messer, S.B., Sass, L.A. & Woolfolk, R.L. (eds.) (1988) *Hermeneutics and Psychological Theory*. New Brunswick and London: Rutgers University Press.

Michon, John (1986) De internationalisering van de Nederlandse psychologie (interview). In: Koenis & Plantenga (red.), 114-124.

Miller, Alice (1984) *Thou Shalt Not Be Aware*. New York: Farrar, Strauss & Giroux.

Mittenzwey, Kuno (1912) Versuch zu einer Darstellung und Kritik der Freudschen Neurosenlehre. *Zeitschrift für Pathopsychologie* 1, 164-186, 369-421, 640-700.

Mooij, A.W.M. (1982) Psychoanalyse als interpretatieve wetenschap. In: *Psychoanalyse en regels*, 85-102. Meppel: Boom.

Morawski, J.G. & Goldstein, S.E. (1985) Psychology and Nuclear War. A Chapter in Our Legacy of Social Responsibility. *American Psychologist* 40, 276-284.

Nelson, J.S. & Megill, A. (1986) Rhetoric of Inquiry: Projects and Prospects. *Quarterly Journal of Speech* 72, 20-37.

Nelson, J.S., Megill, A. & McCloskey, D.N. (eds.) (1987) *The Rhetoric of the Human Sciences*. Madison: The University of Wisconsin Press.

Nisbett, R. & Ross, L. (1980) *Human Inference: Strategies and Shortcomings of Social Judgment*. Englewood Cliffs: Prentice Hall.

Noy, P. (1969) A Revision of the Psychoanalytic Theory of the Primary Process. *International Journal of Psychoanalysis* 50, 155-178.

Nunberg, H. & Federn, E. (eds) (1967) *Minutes of the Vienna Psychoanalytic Society*. New York: International Universities Press.

Orne, M.T. & Holland, C.H. (1968) On the Ecological Validity of Laboratory Deceptions. In: Miller, A.G. (ed.) (1972) *The Social Psychology of Psychological Research*. New York: The Free Press, 122-137.

Oudemans, Th.C.W. (1984) Hermeneutiek: metaforisch spel van binnen en buiten. *Ned.Theol.Tijdschr.* 38, 179-196.

Oudemans, Th.C.W. (1988) Gadamers wijsgerige interpretatieleer. In: Th. de Boer e.a. (red.) *Hermeneutiek*. Meppel: Boom, 54-89.

Oudemans, Th.C.W. & De Jong, R.D. (1983) *Over de natuur van mensen. Inleiding in de filosofische antropologie*. Alphen a/d Rijn/Brussel: Samsom.

Oudemans, Th.C.W. & Lardinois, A.P.M.H. (1987) *Tragic Ambiguity. Anthropology, Philosophy and Sophocles' Antigone*. Leiden/New York: E.J. Brill.

Packer, Martin J. (1985) Hermeneutic Inquiry in the Study of Human Conduct. *American Psychologist* 40, 1081-93.

Parisi, Thomas (1987) Why Freud Failed. Some Implications for Neurophysiology and Sociobiology. *American Psychologist* 42, 235-245.

Peters, R.S. (1958) *The Concept of Motivation*. London: Routledge & Kegan Paul.

Peters, D.P. & Ceci, S.J. (1982) Peer-Review Practices of Psychological Journals: the Fate of Published Articles, Submitted Again. *The Behavioral and Brain Sciences* 5, 187-255.

Peterson, Gerald L. (1981) Historical Self-understanding in the Social Sciences: The Use of Thomas Kuhn in Psychology. *Journal of the Theory of Social Behavior* 11, 1-30.

Piron, H.T. (1965) De Idolen van Linschoten. *Nederlands Tijdschrift voor de Psychologie* 20, 645-654.

Pivik, R. (1978) Tonic states and phasic events in relation to sleep mentation. In: Arkin, A. et al (eds.), *The Mind in Sleep*. Hillsdale, N.J.: Erlbaum, 245-271.

Pool, Robert (1989) Is It Chaos, or Is It Just Noise? *Science* 243, 25-28.

Popper, K.R. (1934) *The Logic of Scientific Discovery*. London: Hutchinson, 1959.

Popper, K. (1961) Facts, Standards and Truth: A Further Criticism of Relativism. Addendum in *The Open Society and its Enemies*, Volume II, 369-396. London: Routledge.

Popper, K.R. (1963) *Conjectures and Refutations*. London: Routledge.

Popper, Karl (1967) La Rationalité et le Statut du Principe de Rationalité. In: Claassen, E.M. (ed.), *Les Fondements Philosophiques des Systèmes Economiques*. Paris: Payot, 142-150.

Popper, K.R. (1970) Normal Science and its Dangers. In: Lakatos, I. & Musgrave, A. (eds.) *Criticism and the Growth of Knowledge.* Cambridge: Cambridge University Press, 51-58.

Popper, K.R. (1974) 'Autobiography of Karl Popper' and 'Replies to My Critics', in: P.A. Schilpp (ed.), *The Philosophy of Karl Popper.* LaSalle, Ill.: Open Court.

Popper, Karl R. (1983) Demarcation: A Case of Verificationism (Psychoanalysis). In: *Realism and the Aim of Science. Postscript to the Logic of Scientific Discovery*, Vol. I. London: Hutchinson, 162-174.

Revesz, G. (1947) *Die Bedeutung der Psychologie für die Praxis und die akademische Ausbildung der Psychologen.* Bern: A. Francke Verlag.

Ricoeur, Paul (1965) *Freud and Philosophy.* New Haven: Yale University Press, 1970.

Roazen, Paul (1975) *Freud and his Followers.* Harmondsworth: Penguin, 1979.

Roe, Rob (1989a) Over welke mensen gaat psychology eigenlijk? *De Psycholoog* 24, 67-73.

Roe, Rob (1989b) Een serieuze zaak. Reactie op Wilke, Koele en De Thouars. *De Psycholoog* 24, 135-139.

Roes, Frans L. (1985) *Wetten in de sociale wetenschappen.* Assen: Van Gorcum.

Royce, Joseph R. (ed.) (1970) *Toward Unification in Psychology. The First Banff Conference on Theoretical Psychology.* Toronto: University of Toronto Press.

Runyan, William McKinley (1982) *Life Histories and Psychobiography. Explorations in Theory and Method.* New York: Oxford University Press.

Rycroft, Charles (1979). *The Innocence of Dreams.* New York: Pantheon Books.

Ryle, G. (1949) *The Concept of Mind.* London: Hutchinson.

Samelson, F. (1980) J.B. Watson's Little Albert, Cyril Burt's Twins and the Need for a Critical Science. *American Psychologist* 35, 619-625.

Samelson, F. (1981) Struggle for Scientific Authority: The Reception of Watson's Behaviorism, 1913-1920. *J. Hist. Behav. Sci.* 17, 399-425.

Sand, R. (1983) Confirmation in the Dora Case. *Int. Rev. Psycho-Anal.* 10, 333-357.

Sanders, C. & Van Rappard, J.F.H. (1987) *Filosofie van de psychologische wetenschappen.* Leiden: Martinus Nijhoff.

Sarbin, Theodore R. (ed.) (1986) *Narrative Psychology. The Storied Nature of Human Conduct.* New York: Praeger.

Sass, Louis A. (1988) Humanism, Hermeneutics, and the Concept of the Human Subject. In: Messer, S.B., et al (eds.), *Hermeneutics and Psychological Theory.* New Brunswick: Rutgers U.P., 222-271.

Savodnik, I. (1976) Is undergoing psychoanalysis essential for the appraisal of psychoanalytic theory? *Inquiry* 19, 299-323.

Schatzman, Morton (1973) *Soul Murder; Persecution in the Family.* London: Allen Lane.

Schenk, Frederieke (1982) De Utrechtse school. De geschiedenis van de Utrechtse psychologie tussen 1945-1965. *Utrechtse historische cahiers* 3, no. 2.

Schick, Paul (1965) *Karl Kraus in Selbstzeugnissen und Bilddokumenten.* Reinbek: Rowohlt.

Schlenker, B.R. (1974) Social Psychology and Science. *J. of Pers. Soc. Psych.* 29, 1-15.

Schnitzler, Arthur (1900) Frau Berta Garlan. *Das erzählerische Werk, Band 2*, 73-196. Frankfurt: Fischer Verlag, 1977.

Schnitzler, Arthur (1925) *Traumnovelle.* Frankfurt: S. Fischer Verlag, 1981.

Schnitzler, A. (1975) Vier unveröffentlichte Briefe Arthur Schnitzlers an den Psychoanalytiker Theodor Reik. *Modern Austrian Literature* 8, 237-.

Schnitzler, A. (1976) Über Psychoanalyse. *Protokolle* 2, 277-284.

Schorske, Carl E. (1980) Politics and Patricide in Freud's Interpretation of Dreams. In: *Fin-de-Siecle Vienna. Politics and Culture.* London: Weidenfeld & Nicholson.

Schultz, J.H. (1909) Psychoanalyse. Die Breuer-Freudschen Lehren, ihre Entwicklung und Aufnahme. *Zeitschrift für angewandte Psychologie und psychologische Sammelforschung* 2, 440-497.

Schusdek, A. (1966) Freud's "Seduction Theory": A Reconstruction. *Journal of the History of the Behavioral Sciences* 2, 159-166.

Schutz, A. (1962) *Collected Papers* I. Den Haag: Nijhoff.

Searle, J.R. (1969) *Speech Acts*. Cambridge: Cambridge University Press.
Segar, Kenneth (1973) Determinism and Character: Arthur Schnitzler's Traumnovelle and his Unpublished Critique of Psychoanalysis. *Oxford German Studies* 8, 114-127.
Seiffert, H. (1975) *Einführung in die Wissenschaftstheorie*. (Band I, II, III). Munich: C.H. Beck.
Seligman, Martin E.P. & Yellen, Amy (1987) What is a Dream? *Behav.Res.Ther.* 25, 1-24.
Sharpe, R.A. (1986) Psychoanalysis, Science or Insight? *Inquiry* 29, 121-132
Sharpe, R.A. (1987) Psychoanalysis and Narrative: A Structuralist Approach. *Int. Rev. Psycho-Anal.* 14, 335-342.
Sharpe, R.A. (1988) Mirrors, Lamps, Organisms and Texts. In: P. Clark & C. Wright, *Mind, Psychoanalysis and Science*. Oxford: Basil Blackwell, 187-203.
Skarda, Christine A. & Freeman, Walter J. (1987) How Brains Make Chaos in Order to Make Sense of the World. *Behavioral and Brain Sciences* 10, 161-173.
Sloane, Paul (1979) *Psychoanalytic Understanding of the Dream*. New York: Jason Aronson.
Smith, Laurence D. (1986) *Behaviorism and Logical Positivism. A Reassessment of the Alliance*. Stanford: Stanford University Press.
Spanjaard, Jacob (1969) The Manifest Dream Content and its Significance for the Interpretation of Dreams. *Int. J. of Psychoanalysis*, 50, 221-235.
Spanjaard, J. (1988) *Over dromen en grootheidswanen*. Meppel: Boom.
Spence, D.P. (1983) Narrative Persuasion. *Psychoanalysis and Contemporary Thought* 6, 457-481.
Staats, Arthur W. (1983) *Psychology's Crisis of Disunity. Philosophy and Method for a Unified Science*. New York: Praeger.
Staats, A.W. et al (1988) Constructing Unified Theory: Methodology from Philosophies in Biological and Psychological Science. Symposium Issue, *Int. Newsletter of Uninomic Psychology* 4, 1-42.
Stam, H.J., Rogers, T.B. & Gergen, K.J. (eds.) (1987) *The Analysis of Psychological Theory. Metapsychological Perspectives*. Washington: Hemisphere.

States, Bert O. (1988) *The Rhetoric of Dreams*. Ithaca: Cornell University Press.

Stekel, W. (Hrsg.) (1913) Varia: Aphorismen über die Pychoanalyse (von Karl Kraus). *Zentrallblatt für Psychoanalyse und Psychotherapie* 3, nr. 12, September 1913, 640-642.

Strasser, S. (1962) *Fenomenologie en empirische menskunde*. Deventer: Van Loghum Slaterus (1970^3).

Strenger, Carlo (1986) Book Review: The Foundations of Psychoanalysis by A. Grünbaum. *Int. J. Psycho-Anal.* 67, 255-260.

Strien, P.J. van (1986) *Praktijk als wetenschap. Methodologie van het sociaal-wetenschappelijk handelen*. Assen: Van Gorcum.

Sulloway, Frank J. (1979) *Freud, Biologist of the Mind*. London: Burnett Books.

Swan, J. (1974) Mater and nannie: Freud's two mothers and the discovery of the Oedipus complex. *American Imago* 31, 1-64.

Szasz, Thomas (1977) *Karl Kraus and the Soul-Doctors*. London: Routledge & Kegan Paul.

Taylor, C. (1964) *The Explanation of Behaviour*. New York: The Humanities Press.

Taylor, C. (1971) Interpretation and the Sciences of Man. *Review of Metaphysics* 25, 3-51. (Reprinted in: Dallmayr, F. & McCarthy, Th. (eds.) *Understanding and Social Inquiry*. Notre Dame University Press 1977, 101-131.)

Taylor, Donald H. (1976) Accidents, Risks, and Models of Explanation. *Human Factors* 18, 371-380.

Taylor, Donald H. (1987) The Hermeneutics of Accidents and Safety. In: J. Rasmussen, K. Duncan & J. Leplat (eds.), *New Technology and Human Error*. London: John Wiley, 31-41.

Terwee, Sybe (1980) The Grammar of Freud's Interpretation of Action. In: R. Haller (ed), *Language, Logic and Philosophy*. Vienna: Pichler-Holder-Temsky, 406-410.

Terwee, S.J.S. (1983) Contextual Theory. In: Harré and Lamb (eds.), *The Encyclopedic Dictionary of Psychology*. Oxford: Basil Blackwell.

Terwee, Sybe (1987/1988) De receptie van Freuds interpretatiekunst. *Psychoanalytisch Forum* 5/4, 6-30; 6/1, 6-35.

Terwee, Sybe (1987a) Het essentialisme van Johannes Linschoten. *Psychologie en Maatschappij* 11, 24-44.

Terwee, S.J.S. (1987b) Grünbaum's Foundations of Psychoanalysis. *Psychoanalysis and Contemporary Thought* 10, 347-372.

Terwee, Sybe (1988a) Need Rhetorical Analysis Lead to Relativism? An Examination of the Views of K.J. Gergen. In: W. Baker et al (eds.), *Recent Trends in Theoretical Psychology*. New York: Springer, 15-27.

Terwee, Sybe (1988b) The Early Reception of Psychoanalysis: Vicissitudes of a Science of Interpretation. In: S. Bem & H. van Rappard (eds.), *Studies in the History of Psychology and the Social Sciences*, Volume 5. Leiden, 48-64.

Terwee, S.J.S. (1990) De beide methodologische hoofdstromen. In: J.F.H. van Rappard & P.J. van Strien (red.), *Grondvragen van de psychologie*. Assen: Van Gorcum.

Terwee, S. (in preparation) *Hermeneutiek in de menswetenschappen*. Meppel: Boom.

Tholey, Paul (1982) Signifikanztest und Bayessche Hypothesenprüfung. *Archiv der Psychologie* 134, 319-342.

Tholey, Paul (1988) A Model for Lucidity Training as a Means of Self-Healing and Psychological Growth. In: J. Gackenbach & S.P. LaBerge (eds), *Conscious Mind, Sleeping Brain. Perspectives on Lucid Dreaming*, 263-287. New York: Plenum Press.

Tholey, P. & Utecht, K. (1988) *Bewust willen dromen*. Naarden: Strengholt.

Toulmin, S. (1954) The logical status of psychoanalysis. In: M. MacDonald (ed.), *Philosophy and Analysis*. New York: Philosophical Library.

Toulmin, Stephen & Leary, David E. (1985) The Cult of Empiricism in Psychology, and Beyond. In: Koch, S. & Leary, D. (eds.), *A Century of Psychology as a Science*, 594-617.

Tribbia, J.J. & Anthes, R.A. (1987). Scientific Basis of Modern Weather Prediction. *Science* 237, 493-499.

Tritton, David (1986) Chaos in the swing of a pendulum. *New Scientist* 24/7, 37-40.

Urbach, P. (1974) Progress and Degeneration in the IQ-Debate. *Brit. J. Phil. Science* 25, 99-136 & 235-259.

Urban, B. (1978) Schnitzler and Freud as doubles: *The Psychoanal.Rev.* 65, 131-153.

Veldkamp, Tjibbe Anne & Van Drunen, Peter (1988) *Psychologie als professie.* Assen: Van Gorcum.

Vlek, Charles & Wagenaar, Willem A. (1979) Judgment and decision under uncertainty. In: John A. Michon et al., *Handbook of Psychonomics.* Amsterdam: North-Holland, 253-345.

Vlek, Charles (1987) Psychologische besliskunde. Tussen weddenschaps-wetenschap en professionele beslissingsondersteuning. *De Psycholoog* 22, 73-86.

Vogel, Gerald W. (1978). An Alternative View of the Neurobiology of Dreaming. *American Journal of Psychiatry* 135, 1531-35.

Vries, G. de (1984) *De ontwikkeling van wetenschap.* Groningen: Wolters-Noordhoff. (Tweede, gewijzigde druk: 1985).

Vries, G.H. de (1986) W.K.B. Hofstee over 'De ontwikkeling van wetenschap'. *Nederlands Tijdschrift voor de Psychologie* 41, 97-99.

Vroon, P. & Draaisma, D. (1985) *De mens als metafoor.* Baarn: Ambo.

Wagenaar, Willem A. (1986a) My Memory: A Study of Autobiographical Memory over Six Years. *Cognitive Psychology* 18, 225-252.

Wagenaar, W.A. (1986b) *De oorzaak van onmogelijke ongelukken.* Deventer: Van Loghum Slaterus.

Wagenaar, W.A. (1987a) Reflectie op zijreflectie. *NRC-Handelsblad*, Febr. 12, 1987.

Wagenaar, W.A. (1987b) Logisch voorwaarts en intelligent terugwaarts: modellen voor het stellen van diagnoses. In: Crombag e.a., *De psychologie voorbij*, pp. 83-92.

Wagenaar, W.A. (1987c) Nawoord: De constructie van risico. *Nederlands Tijdschrift voor de Psychologie* 42, 53-54.

Wagenaar, W.A. & Keren, G.B. (1986) The Seat Belt Paradox: Effect of Adapted Roles on Information Seeking. *Organisational Behavior and Human Decision Processes* 38, 1-6.

Wagenaar, W.A. & Groeneweg, J. (1987) Accidents at sea. Multiple causes and impossible consequences. *Int. J. of Man-Machine Studies* 27, 587-598.

Westenberg, Mirjam (1988) High Utili-Tea in Cambridge. Verslag van het elfde SPUDM-congres. *De Psycholoog* 23, 60-61.

White, P. (1980) Limitation on Verbal Reports of Internal Events: A Refutation of Nisbett and Wilson and of Bem. *Psychological Review* 87, 105-112.

Widdershoven, Guy (1987) *Handelen en rationaliteit.* Meppel: Boom.

Wijngaarden, H.R. (1985) *Luisteren naar dromen.* Meppel: Boom.

Will, David (1986) Psychoanalysis and the new Philosophy of Science. *Int.Rev.Psycho-Anal.* 13, 163-173.

Willbern, David (1979) Freud and the Inter-Penetration of Dreams. *Diacritics* 9, 98-110.

Wittels, F. (1967) Die "Fackel"-Neurose. Paper read on 12-1-1910, Vienna Psychoanalytic Society. In: H. Nunberg and E. Federn (eds.), *Minutes of the Vienna Psychoanalytic Society, Vol. II*, 382-393, New York.

Wittgenstein, L. (1922) *Tractatus Logico-philosophicus.* London: Routledge and Kegan Paul.

Wittgenstein, Ludwig (1953) *Philosophical Investigations* (PI). Oxford: Basil Blackwell.

Wittgenstein, L. (1958) *The Blue and Brown Books.* Oxford: Basil Blackwell.

Wittgenstein, Ludwig (1969) *On Certainty* (OC). Oxford: Basil Blackwell.

Wittgenstein, Ludwig (1977) *Culture and Value.* (translation of: Vermischte Bemerkungen). Oxford: Basil Blackwell, 1980.

Wolters, Gezinus & Phaf, R. Hans (1988). Connectionisme: een nieuwe uitdaging voor de psychologie. *De Psycholoog* 23, 361-369.

Woolfolk, R.L., et al (1988) Introduction to Hermeneutics. In: Messer et al (eds.) *Hermeneutics and Psychological Theory*, pp. 2-26.

Wright, G.H. von (1971) *Explanation and Understanding.* London: Routledge and Kegan Paul.

Zeeman, E.C. (1976) Catastrophe Theory. *Scientific American* 234, 65-83.

NAME INDEX

SUBJECT INDEX

GPSR Compliance

The European Union's (EU) General Product Safety Regulation (GPSR) is a set of rules that requires consumer products to be safe and our obligations to ensure this.

If you have any concerns about our products, you can contact us on ProductSafety@springernature.com

In case Publisher is established outside the EU, the EU authorized representative is:

Springer Nature Customer Service Center GmbH
Europaplatz 3
69115 Heidelberg, Germany

Batch number: 10844675

Printed by Printforce, the Netherlands